Nellie and Charlie

✦

A Family Memoir of the Gilded Age

Helen Tower Brunet

Helen Tower Brunet

iUniverse, Inc.
New York Lincoln Shanghai

Nellie and Charlie
A Family Memoir of the Gilded Age

iUniverse books may be ordered through booksellers or by contacting:

iUniverse
2021 Pine Lake Road, Suite 100
Lincoln, NE 68512
www.iuniverse.com
1-800-Authors (1-800-288-4677)

ISBN: 0-595-34384-8

Printed in the United States of America

Nellie and Charlie

With love to my grandchildren—Samantha, George, Elizabeth, Sarah, Margaret and Catherine.

Contents

Acknowledgements

I would like to thank my family who encouraged me to write this book: my husband, Stuart, who patiently read every version of every chapter and my three children, Geoffrey, Stuart and Pamela whose enthusiasm for this project kept me going. In addition, my son Stuart provided hours of technical support from his computer in California to mine here in the East.

My thanks also to my cousins, Gertrude Dodson and Helen Wilson, who shared family papers they had stored for years, and to my daughter-in-law, Mary R. Brunet, who mapped Nellie's travels around old California. I am grateful to three friends who patiently read earlier versions of the book and made good suggestions—Joan White, Marilyn Setzer and Ann Nash.

I am especially grateful to Sidney C. Moody, a writer and editor of long experience, for reading the manuscript line by line

Preface

I was born in the Tower Homestead, a white frame Greek Revival house in the village of Waterville, in upstate New York, near the towns of Hamilton and Clinton. The house had been in the Tower family for four generations. When my father, Geoffrey, the second son of Nellie and Charlemagne Tower, inherited the house at Nellie's death in 1931, Geoffrey was still a bachelor. It would be several years before he married and moved to Waterville, where he planned to make a living raising horses.

Growing up in the Tower Homestead, I was aware of the earlier generations who had lived there. The attic was filled with memorabilia dating back to the early 1800's, and some of the furnishings had not been changed since my great-grandparents time. We didn't live in a state of ancestor worship as much as ancestor awareness.

I was selectively interested in the family lore, especially the awe-inspiring story of my father's great-grandfather, Reuben Tower, who rode horseback from Waterville to St. Augustine, Florida in 1834, in the hope that a warm climate would cure his tuberculosis. It took him three months and, unfortunately, he died a few months after his arrival in St. Augustine.

Another ancestor story that captured my imagination concerned my paternal grandmother, Nellie Smith, who, while on a cruise to Alaska with her father, met a mysterious stranger (who later became my grandfather). By the age of eleven, when I had broadened my interests from horses and farm animals to include love stories, especially the radio soap opera *Our Gal Sunday,* I realized that there were certain parallels between Sunday and Nellie.

The orphan from the little mining town of Silver Creek, Colorado, married "a wealthy and titled Englishman." Nellie, from Oakland, California, would marry Charlemagne Tower, junior, a wealthy young man from the East whom I was sure was on a par with Lord Henry Brinthrope.

I began making secret forays into the attic to rummage through old trunks in search of Nellie's love letters and diaries. What I found instead was a jumble of ancient documents, maps, and ledgers from a long ago distillery business. The only packet of letters I found was from my great-great-grandmother, Deborah Tower, to her husband, Reuben, (who would later ride the horse to Florida) who was in the New York State Militia fighting at Sackett's Harbor on Lake Champlain during the War of 1812. Deborah was furious at Reuben (whom she addressed as Husband) for extending his commission and leaving her alone in the middle of winter. The cow was going dry which threatened her supply of butter needed to barter for firewood. And their two little boys were sick with whooping cough. These were hardly the love letters I sought.

Then one day I found Nellie's journal of her trip to Alaska, a small black leather diary, bound with red satin ribbon. The little lined pages were covered with spidery writing that flowed across the pages and then up into the margins. Nellie wrote in detail of the trip and her excitement when she met "Mr. Tower." I was enthralled, and started searching in earnest for possible love letters, but I never found more than a few of Nellie's possessions and mementoes in the attic.

Years later, after the house in Waterville had been sold, and my mother and father had died, I sorted through my share of the treasures from the attic which included most of the trunks I used to love poking around in so long ago. At last, I thought, I could really pull the trunks apart and find the rest of the diaries and letters that I felt sure she must have written. Surely she would have saved mementoes of her family life with my grandfather and their five children. But I found nothing more about Nellie and Charlemagne until four years ago.

I was at a dinner party when my host, Jim Porter, showed me a book his wife, Katie, had given him for Christmas, *Water for Gotham,* by Gerard Koeppel, which mentioned one of my early ancestors, Fayette Bartholomew Tower. Fayette, the fourth of Deborah and Reuben's eight children, grew up in the Tower Homestead and as a young man served as an engineer on the Croton Aqueduct. I thumbed through the book with interest and found in the credits that many papers about my father's family had been loaned to the author by my distant cousin, Helen Tower Wilson.

When I located her in New Mexico, she told me she had a large collection of letters and clippings about my grandparents stacked in boxes in her garage and would happily send them to me.

The missing pieces of the lives of my grandparents arrived in huge boxes a few days later. There were letters, pictures, newspaper clippings and several more diaries, as well as four enormous scrapbooks in which Nellie had recorded my grandfather's diplomatic career.

When I had almost finished writing this book, another wonderful coincidence occurred. My first cousin, Gertrude Dodson, called from Washington D.C. to tell me that she had found two more of our grandmother's diaries, one written the year before Nellie took the cruise, and one written just after, which included the engagement period—and there were thirty letters written by Nellie and Charlie to each other during their coast-to-coast courtship. I had found the love letters at last.

As I reconstructed their lives, the story that I had always thought of as the happily-ever-after tale of two Victorians who met by chance, married for love, lived in palaces in Europe and America and had five perfect children, became a much more interesting story of the lives of real people.

Helen Tower Brunet, Mendham, New Jersey

1

Nellie Smith, Spinster, 1886

There were times during the long summer of 1886 when Nellie Smith thought nothing in her life would ever change. She was almost twenty-eight years old and still had not met the right man. She longed to travel to exotic places, but seldom went farther than the ferry ride from her home in Oakland, California, across the bay to San Francisco. She confided her frustrations to her diary and endured the long, lazy, days at the family ranch in the California Sierra Mountains.

Nellie's summer had gotten off to a slow start. In June, her mother took two of her sisters, Ada and Gertrude, on a cruise to Alaska, leaving Nellie in charge of moving her aunt and her youngest brother, Cecil, to the ranch.

Nellie would rather have stayed in Oakland with her father, Frank Smith, an attorney who practiced in San Francisco, and her brothers Bert and Percy, who had jobs in the city. She knew, however, that was out of the question.

Her family thought it entirely fair that Nellie should run the household at the ranch while her mother took Gertrude and Ada on the cruise, since Nellie had accompanied her father on a trip to San Diego, California, the previous winter.

But to Nellie, as much as she adored her father, five days in southern California hardly equaled a three-week trip to Alaska. Feeling like a martyr, she wrote in her diary: "I had a noble feeling…that I had made a sacrifice cheerfully by coming here to the ranch—thus enabling Mama, Ada and Gertrude to get off to Alaska…I was following their trip with the Alaska map along the wall with great assiduity and counting the days until they should join us."

Nellie's responsibilities at the ranch included supervising the kitchen help and keeping her elderly Aunt Sallie company in her mother's absence. She also read aloud for several hours a day to her thirteen-year-old brother, Cecil, who had been partially blinded by scarlet fever. This was more a pleasure than a duty because Cecil was quick, amusing and interested in everything.

When the travelers returned from Alaska at the end of June, Nellie's sister Ada, an artist, went with friends on a sketching trip to Bolinas Bay on the coast.

1

Nellie and her sister Gertrude settled into the often tedious routines of summer at the ranch, a rustic mountain retreat where the emphasis was on the benefits of fresh air in a tranquil setting.

It was that very tranquility which so bored Nellie and Gertrude. When the family had first started going to the ranch they were all together for the whole summer: Nellie, her brothers Bert, Percy and little Cecil, her sisters Ada and Gertrude and even her oldest sister, Floie, who came with her new husband, LeRoy, for part of the summer. Nellie remembered those early summers with longing. Bert and Percy were forever dreaming up new adventures. The house rang with laughter.

Now summer at the ranch was just plain tedious. She wrote in her diary: "Oh! Life has become so tiresome to me and after Gertrude and I are in bed at night we tally off one more day gone. There are no recreations here, nothing to amuse ourselves with. This constant inactivity is very wearying."

Nellie and Gertrude read, worked on their embroidery, wrote letters, walked, and played badminton during the day. In the evening they played whist, their favorite card game.

The summer days inched by until September 2, Nellie's twenty-eighth birthday. The day began with a birthday breakfast, a family tradition, with her mother presiding at the big table in the rustic dining room. Around it were Aunt Sallie, Gertrude, and Cecil, as well as Floie who had arrived at the ranch in August with her three small children, Gladys, Amy and Harold.

Nellie opened her mother's gift first, a new diary, bound in red leather. She was delighted to see that members of her family, including those absent, had already filled in the first ten pages. Each entry was a birthday tribute to Nellie, in the form of a poem or letter. Ada had sent two small watercolor paintings of Bolinas Bay on the coast, that were inserted in the back pages of the diary. Family custom dictated that each tribute be read aloud. Nellie later described the happy day in her new diary:

> A new journal—a new year…I had such a happy birthday, one of the loveliest I ever remember.
>   I do hope it is the foreshadow of the coming year…Cecil had made for me…a string of acorns shaped into baskets made by his own dear hands using a dull knife. It is nearly two yards long—a precious souvenir of his patience yet pleasure—probably three-hundred baskets, each one will indicate to me a separate thought of the summer…Mama gave me five dollars with which I intend to have the beautiful fox skin dressed that was brought me by them from Alaska. The little Harvey family gave me an exquisite white handker-

chief. Aunt Sallie handed me a sweet little note and five dollars to buy a souvenir of the day which will probably be a book. Ada to my delighted surprise sent me a beautiful sketch of Bolinas Bay—also two small watercolors on two letters, and a lovely fancy bag containing a little bag for needles, thimble and buttons—it was all to be used for travelling…Immediately after breakfast, we prepared lunch…

By l0 a.m. we were all off—Gladys, Amy and Harold on horseback—Cecil and one of we girls dragging Gladys's wagon containing lunch, fancywork, books, etc. Mama and Aunt Sallie kept the lead and looked like twins indeed with their red and blue parasols. Floie made a comical picture at one time protecting herself, children and her horse from a slowly advancing cow, by a club twice as big as herself. It was a lovely spot on the creek by the mill. Cecil was charmed with the singing rush of the water and was very content all day…We all read aloud together…We had a merry lunch.

Some of us walked to the mill later—such lovely bunches of golden sunlight and shadow covered the dear pines. While Mama and Aunt Sallie walked around the mill Gertie and I sat down alone and had one of our dear sweet talks. A watermelon was passed around at 3, then Floie floated half of it down the stream to read in its passage my future life. It went smoothly on its course with a little help once from Gertrude and once from Harold…

The others all left at 5 pm but Gertie and I begged for another hour. We talked of our whist club next winter…what we wanted our husbands to be like and hundreds of things that only two devoted hearts and most congenial souls ever dare touch upon! Then we walked home.

A few weeks later when it was finally time to go home, Nellie and Gertrude couldn't wait to begin the long day's journey back to Oakland, first by horse drawn carriage and then by train.

The three-story house on Castro Street always seemed to Nellie both spacious and wonderfully luxurious compared to the Spartan accommodations at the ranch. Now she saw the city around her with new eyes, admiring the streets shaded with old oak trees and sidewalks bordered with intricately patterned wrought iron fences enclosing bountiful gardens. Their own garden, she later wrote in a diary, was filled with rare trees, "camellias…India rubber, bamboo, cinnamon, magnolia, orange and heliotrope."

The Smiths had moved to Oakland from San Francisco in 1881 after Cecil's bout with scarlet fever, in hopes of finding cleaner, healthier air across the bay. Land values in the developing city of Oakland were good and large homes were less expensive than in San Francisco.

The population of Oakland had burgeoned after 1869 when it became the terminus for the first transcontinental railroad. By the 1880's, Oakland was not only a thriving port city, but also a center of commerce and industry with good schools and the beginnings of a strong civic pride. Regular ferry service offered an easy commute to San Francisco.

Nellie, a graduate of the Snell Seminary for Young Ladies in Oakland, devoted part of her time to good works. She strived to practice the tenets of Victorian womanhood: selfless devotion to family and community and a strong commitment to self-improvement. She was president of the Fruit and Flower Mission that raised money for the poor. She visited elderly family friends on a regular basis, and often took over the management of the family home for her mother, who at times suffered from poor health.

Nellie read uplifting texts and kept lists of the books she read. She worked to perfect her skills at painting, embroidery and other decorative arts, as well as singing and playing the piano.

The greatest pleasure for Nellie and her sisters were their trips to San Francisco for theater, concerts or shopping. Nellie attended a Saturday morning French class at the home of Mrs. Colton, a close family friend who lived on Nob Hill. Studying French fueled Nellie's dreams of foreign travel.

Nellie came by her love of travel from her father, Frank Smith, born in Jamaica of English parents. Frank's father, a plantation owner in Jamaica, was a retired English army officer. As a boy Frank, whose full name was George Francis Smith, briefly studied for the priesthood at a Jesuit school run by the College of St. John in the West Indies. After a few years he decided instead to study law and went to England to school at Bruce Castle near London. The school, run by a Mr. Hill, specialized in progressive education. Frank later studied law in London.

It was on a visit to the United States in the early 1850's, that Frank Smith met and fell in love with Susan Rising in New York. Susan's family, originally from Grafton, Massachusetts, numbered among their forebears at least one passenger on the Mayflower.

Soon after they were married, Frank and Susan made the trip West via Panama, eventually settling in San Francisco where Frank was admitted to the California bar in 1854 and began the practice of law.

In 1887, Nellie was not the only member of the family who craved change. Bert and Percy, who had been unable to find good jobs in San Francisco, were planning to go to South America.

2

A Sea Voyage

By the middle of the winter of 1887, Bert and Percy had decided to seek their fortunes in Guatemala, Bert in the telephone business and Percy in ice manufacture. Their impending departure was wrenching for Nellie's close-knit family.

The whole family turned out to say goodbye on the day of departure. Nellie later wrote in her diary that as they walked down the gangplank to their waiting ship she cried as she watched from the dock.

> Oh! How I envied them—Oh! Journal dear I know it is wicked of me but I do so despise Oakland and am so sick of San Francisco that it seems to me I cannot tolerate another ten years more here…What will home be without them?

Nellie's spirits lifted a month later when it was decided that she and her father would take a cruise to Alaska, leaving San Francisco in early June. She and her sisters set about preparing her travel wardrobe in a state of high excitement.

Nellie knew that the trip would put a strain on her father's precarious finances, but her father was determined to go. He told Nellie he thought the cost was reasonable considering the distance they would travel and the luxury of the steamer *Olympian*. He intended to write an account of the voyage that he would submit to the *San Francisco Chronicle* or an Oakland newspaper and if he were paid for it, it would help defray some of the cost of the trip.

In the back of his mind, no doubt, was the thought that Nellie might meet a suitable young man. Travel, properly chaperoned, was the approved way for a young woman to broaden her acquaintanceship.

That Nellie was twenty-eight years old and still not married perplexed her parents. Although not beautiful, she was sweet looking, her face surrounded by chestnut curls. She was slender, vivacious and charming, and always a perfect lady.

Frank and Susan Smith tried to provide opportunities for their three unmarried daughters to meet eligible bachelors, but still only Floie was married. A few years earlier General Murphy, a younger friend of Frank Smith's who owned a large ranch in Santa Margarita had expressed an interest in Nellie. He was charming, but Nellie felt no spark, and the matter was dropped.

Nellie had a large circle of devoted friends her own age, but the group included few suitable bachelors, except her dear friend William Keith. An accomplished singer whom she enjoyed accompanying on the piano at parties, "Keithy" unfortunately had few prospects—he had a lowly job as a clerk at a San Francisco department store, and seemed content with that. Nellie longed for much more. She confessed in her diary: "A life of travel is all that has a charm for me—I never could be content settling down with a poor man and the prospect of slaving all my life—never! Never! I could not love enough for that."

When the long-awaited day of departure for Alaska arrived, it got off to a dreary start. Frank Smith had been sick in bed the day before and still felt weak when they boarded the steamer, *George C. Elder*, for the three-day voyage to Victoria, Canada, where they would transfer to the *Olympian* for the journey on to Alaska.

Nellie recorded in her journal:

> The morning that Papa and I started he was miserable, getting up from a sick bed, but the doctor said a sea trip would be the best thing for him…we had three disagreeable days on the *Elder* and would actually have suffered if it had not been for the kindness of Captain Ackley in insisting on giving us the free use of his room and the pilot house. It rained, I felt half sick, had two quiet companions in my room, one carrying into our close quarters an easel and a birdcage…
>
> Once we began advancing towards Victoria I seemed to take a new lease on life. The sun came out and seemed to say to me "brightest dreams await you."

The luxurious new steamer *Olympian* was an entirely different world. Frank Smith described it in a newspaper article he published on his return:

> The luxury and comfort of this vessel is almost beyond description. She is unquestionably the handsomest steamer that has ever been on the Pacific Coast. *The Olympian* has a saloon not inferior in either size or furniture to the grandest parlors of our best hotels, lit entirely by electricity, four sumptuous meals a day, with handsome table appointments and excellent waiters, free bath rooms, large state rooms and exceptionally comfortable beds.

He noted that the cost of the entire trip, twenty-two days round trip from San Francisco, first on the *Elder* and then on the *Olympian*, was $160 for each person.

Nellie was delighted with her luxurious stateroom on the main deck, with two windows, one facing east and one north, as the ship traveled northward.

Tuesday, June 14, 1887. First day on the *Olympian* and my thermometer of happiness is going even higher. The clouds still hang over the sky, it even threatens rain, but everything forebodes a very charming trip.... The water now looks silver, blue and grey, affected by the different currents of air...There seems to be some very pleasant gentlemen, although there is no face in particular to which I have taken a fancy...My seat [at dinner] is next to young Dorsay, but I do not like him at all. He is braggadocio, boorish, old yet young, stupid...Oh! This wild, wild scenery—it makes one feel so happy, so joyous, so good to all the world...after the theatre three gentlemen were talking in the cabin and one raised his eyes to mine and deliberately stared—I thought them three old married men and wondered who better the steamer would show as passengers.

Nellie assumed that the three men were executives of the Northern Pacific Railroad. On the next day, June 15, she recorded in her diary that one of the men stared at her constantly:

At breakfast and at lunch the next day it was the same, his eyes forever on me—in the evening promenading below, I was sitting above in front of the pilot house with Mrs. Paul and Miss Hibbard and felt positively uncomfortable he stared so continuously...in the afternoon he asked Mrs. Paul to present him and I was formally introduced. I stayed with him only a moment, making an excuse to go indoors—but in that moment I heard his voice, it was so educated, so sweet, his manners so charming that I saw I had done him a great injustice. After dinner he joined me again and I was very much interested and began to feel that he was going to make my trip delightful...

He seems to be about 45 or 50, very tall, very homely, sick looking, ungraceful, but pleasant voice and is going to be I think very interesting. His eyes have never left me since I first entered the cabin that first night after the theatre. He sits opposite at the Captain's table and every time I look up his eyes are upon me.

3

Charlie Tower, Bachelor

The man across the table was not an executive of the Northern Pacific Railroad, as Nellie supposed. He was Charlemagne Tower Jr., the only son of Charlemagne Tower of Philadelphia, a major shareholder in the Northern Pacific Railroad.

Charlemagne junior, called Charlie, was thirty-nine years old and still a bachelor. He had for five years been managing his father's interests in the mining of iron ore in Minnesota; his job on this trip was to inspect his father's properties along the path of the Northern Pacific Railroad.

Father and son kept in constant touch by telegram; typically, Charlie would wire his father at the end of the business day and have his father's answer by noon the next day. He sent less urgent information by letter. Charlie reported to his father on the pleasure of the train trip from Duluth to Tacoma in a letter dated June 9, 1887:

> The trip has been delightful in point of enjoyment and very full of information to me; not only as relates to the Northern Pacific Road but as to the resources of this whole country West of the Missouri River and the Rocky Mountains. It is a great world of which we have no conception in the East, and which nobody can believe in without coming to see it for himself...Possibly I ought to except you from this general statement, because I remember that you have always believed in it and what I see now justifies what I have heard you say.

The senior Tower, seventy-eight years old, had been a practicing attorney most of his working life in Pottsville, Pennsylvania. In 1875 he retired and moved to Philadelphia. At the time of his retirement, he was a wealthy man, primarily from successful land speculation.

Charlemagne's many interests in retirement included making improvements on the Tower Homestead in Waterville, New York, where he had grown up and where he and his family now spent the summer, compiling a collection of English common law used in colonial laws which had been a project for a number of years, compiling a genealogy of the Tower family, and a truly grand scheme for a man of his age: the development of iron ore in the Vermilion Iron Range in Minnesota.

During the early years of his father's interest in the Minnesota iron ore venture, Charlie, having graduated from Exeter and Harvard, traveled throughout Europe on a grand tour which lasted more than three years. He visited Spain, France, Germany, Denmark, Norway, Sweden, Russia, Turkey, Jerusalem, Greece and Egypt, a truly impressive itinerary.

Charlemagne, always generous with his four daughters, Deborah, Emma, Henrietta and Grace, went to extra expense for Charlie. He considered travel just as important as formal education. When Charlie returned to Philadelphia in 1876, he read law and passed the Pennsylvania Bar Examination in 1878. In the spring of 1882, Charlie went to Duluth where he managed his father's mining ventures. He supervised the building of the Iron Range railroad for the transportation of iron ore and later served as President of the Duluth and Iron Range Railroad Company and as Managing Director of the Minnesota Iron Company.

In Duluth Charlie worked from morning until night, with very little social life. His father expected him to accomplish things quickly and thoroughly and to keep him informed every step of the way. This meant daily telegrams and two or three lengthy letters to his father each week.

Just days before Nellie and Charlie met on board the *Olympian* in June of 1887, Charlemagne Tower had signed an agreement to sell both the railroad and the mining company to a syndicate, headed by Henry H. Porter of Chicago. Included in the syndicate were J. C. Morse of the Union Steel Company, Marshall Field, and J. D. Rockefeller of the Standard Oil Company. The sale price of the railroad and mining companies and the block of stock he retained in the new company made Charlemagne a millionaire.

At the time of the Alaskan trip Charlie did not know whether he would be offered a position in the new company and thus continue to live in Duluth, or if he would move back to Philadelphia and pursue other interests. Both he and his father hoped that Henry Porter would offer him a position. In any event, Charlie became wealthy from the sale of the railroad and mining companies; he could afford to be very selective in choosing his future career.

On board the *Olympian*, however, the only evidence of wealth that Nellie noticed and recorded in her diary that first day was the presence of Charlie's manservant, an elderly Negro named William. The two men from the Northern Pacific Railroad were the company's president, Charles B. Wright, and another executive of the company, Mr. Brookman. When Wright encouraged Charlie to travel on with them to Alaska on the *Olympian*, Charlie wired his father of his plans and promised to make a detailed inspection of the senior Tower's holdings in the Washington Territory after the cruise.

We have no written record of the Alaskan trip from Charlie's point of view, but in the pages of her diary, Nellie gave a vivid account of her feelings as their friendship developed:

> Thursday, June 16—How I have had to change in my feelings toward Mr. Tower. He is simply charming. He interests me beyond words…His voice is so rich, his manner so finished, so charming and he is such a wonderful listener and splendid story teller…my heart is completely captured. He thinks me "an interesting lovely girl"…
>
> When we went ashore at Sitka, I had his willing hand and strong arm to protect me—his rich, full voice whispered sweet nothings in my ear and I was perfectly happy…we climbed the moraines, gazed about us for a while on the turrets of ice and then joined Papa on the beach…
>
> Saturday, June 18 at Juneau…Mr. Tower and I walked about and he bought me a lovely bracelet which I will keep always as a souvenir of his dear self…He cannot get over it because he had to come this long distance to meet little me—and questions as to what he would do after next Tuesday when I have left him…He speaks of coming to California very soon to see me…
>
> Mr. Tower has decided to go with us to Tacoma and then return to do his business in Victoria later. That made me very joyous. We sat outside after leaving the wharf at Juneau and after a lovely little supper downstairs he fixed me so comfortably in my steamer chair, then moved his very close and then we sat oh so happily together, watching our retreat from Juneau, our last stopping place. He pressed my hand and said what happiness I had brought into his life, that he had never dreamed of such bliss.
>
> Sunday, June 1—I must write just a few lines before I retire in my dear room where I have spent six days…just how happy I have been I will not fully realize until I have returned home and all is over. Mr. Tower and I had the loveliest talk and walk this evening—it was very cold…we could see Fort Longas and little islands with the dancing waves dashing high. It was very wild and oh! How grand to watch the great sea swell and then see ourselves ride over it. We walked and became warm, then sat down and he bundled me all up—told me how perfectly happy he was and I asked him as a personal favor to me to have a talk with Papa and see how wonderfully interesting he was and so the dear man has just taken him outside for a promenade…
>
> Mrs. Evans and Mrs. Paul both told me tonight that he was of such a fine family and that he was worth, with his father, at least six millions. I am glad I have been ignorant of it all this time, otherwise I should not have had such perfect freedom in being with him. I certainly cannot but feel greatly compli-

mented at his extreme attentions—he comes so pointedly to join me on every occasion and then in his rich voice says, "Come, Miss Smith, let us walk." He laughingly pointed out tonight the anchor on which I was sitting the first time he saw me…and that before being introduced he watched me steadily, that I knew…when his eyes were not upon me I supposed they were on some other girl…now I know that he cares for no-one on board but me. My clear eyes are his sunshine, he told me, and when I refused last night for the sixth time to give him my photograph but asked for his—to which he replied, "No, Milady—I cannot let you have it to show exultingly to your California friends and say, 'Here was a slave of mine for four days.'"

I wonder if I ever will see him again. He tells me he is positively coming to California, but alas! I have had so many friends like him before—to charm me for a summer day. Ah! The hours and hours we talk without the least fatigue—with him I feel my true and best self, speaking freely, frankly and sincerely. He is exceptionally interesting.

Victoria, Wednesday June 22. On the *Olympian* at Harbor. Oh! What a perfect two days I have had! I do not see how we could have enjoyed anything more. We saw one glacier on one perfect day…We reached Victoria at 10 a.m. on a beautiful warm, balmy morning.…I wrote letters, Mr. Tower and I chatted…He begged me to go up town with him for a few errands. I did not dream I could, but Papa has been so good all along, and simply told me to return in time for lunch. We had a dear little walk and talk together and he begged me to accept a Japanese fan, one that he had seen and admired at a store. The store was closed, but we returned this a.m. and now it is in my possession, with its pretty pink dangling tassels and embossed sticks…

The sham naval battle [held in honor of Queen Victoria's Jubilee] on land was rather a failure, but Papa and I took a carriage with the Bishop and his wife and enjoyed it socially immensely—Mr. Tower was watching me from his carriage below on the field—I knew it. He stood up in the carriage and watched the whole sham battle which was entertaining but not thrilling and when it was over, we could not tell who had won.

That evening, oh! Happy night…I had the happy consciousness that he was walking up and down by my room until the light was out, and I allowed him to come to my window and shake my hand good night. Then I thought better of it and forbade it, but still he watched outside until he fancied me asleep.

The next morning, alas! He told me he had decided to leave at once—that there would be no particular satisfaction in going to Tacoma, he would have to be so much with the others and the only thing in the world that would take him there would be to see me—that if we never meet again a day or two more or less would amount to nothing. If we did meet again, we would have so much more that this would not be missed.

I said "by all means go—if there lies your duty there is the right step for you to take, and that is to go"—I wondered at my own bravery and cheerfulness, for that meant at once that night, perhaps after that day, never again—but what a day…

Leaving Victoria, 7:20 p.m. He has gone from me—out of my life. Tonight he takes the Canadian Pacific—Oh—He is so lovely—today oh! What happiness for me. He hopes to come to California in September, if not, we will never meet again. What joy he has brought into my life! I must try and be philosophical and take the rest of the trip as tho' I had never met him and have only a feeling of thankfulness that he has brought so much pleasure in my life on this trip—he has not left my side for one moment without asking when he could return.

I told him I would put on my Mary Anderson cloak, the way I was the first night he saw me and stand apart to bid him goodbye. I wisely went on the upper deck and alone I walked. He moved apparently out of sight of all the others on aboard, but from where I stood I could spy him and we saluted hat and fan energetically. Papa joined me again, we waved, and again until we were out of sight—what a lump came into my throat—September or forever! My almost ideal man, one whom at least I must thank for all my pleasure on this boat.

Nellie Smith in 1887. She sent this
picture to Charlie during their
courtship.

Charlie (Charlemagne) Tower in 1887.
This is the picture he sent to
Nellie after the trip to Alaska.

Nellie Smith's home on Castro Street in Oakland, California 1885.

Old Tower Homestead, Waterville, N. Y.

The Tower Homestead in Waterville, New York before the
west wing was added in 1910.

4

Nellie in Love

Nellie's heart was heavy as her ship steamed away from Victoria. She could no longer see Charlie waving from the dock. Why had he suddenly changed his mind about going on to Tacoma with her? Had he received a telegram from his father? Was it because he was spending more time thinking about her than about his father's western properties. She hoped it was the latter. In the privacy of her cabin, she poured out her heart in her diary:

> He is moving further from me every moment. Oh—How I miss my dear, sweet man. I have an idea that he is thinking of me. I wonder, does he miss me—he said so often that he never could get along without me—but oh! He is a man and hence a privileged character…
>
> I never have cared for anyone so much before, and it is so foolish of me because I may never see him again—he thinks he is coming this September…it seems too great a joy to be mine and when I reason how full of business he is and how much attention he must receive, my heart fails me…
>
> He begged for my address that he might write to me. I delayed giving it to tease him, but I knew in my own heart I had not the strength to refuse his pleading…He kept continually saying "what will become of me when you are gone? When I have those dear eyes no more to look into?" I really do not see how I always had the courage to answer him so pertly for he was so dear to me. He has been a man of the world, I, a woman—we both have experiences we never would repeat or ask for in each other, but oh! We are so congenial, so companionable—He used to say "to think I had to come way out to Alaska to meet you, you dear little woman," and then told me how he had not wanted to go but fate led him on—how alike was my experience for did I not put the decision of the steamers, date of departure, everything in Papa's hands? I must become very strong and try to drive him out of my thoughts but oh—life seems so tame to me now…
>
> Does he feel that it was a pleasant little flirtation, or that I am necessary to his happiness! Ah me—I can never like anyone else in all the wide world. He satisfies every thought, feeling, moment and ambition of my wildest

dreams—When we parted he said, "I am the better man for having known you and if I come to California it means absolute surrender…"

How my feelings have changed since the first morning when he handed me a chair and I so scornfully accepted it—let me see, what did I think of him then? That he was a married flirt, his plaid collars made me think, although I knew them to be stylish, that perhaps he was a dry goods man or tailor, and now I think him at times handsome…sweet, even tender, so manly, so much character, very strong will but will yield to good judgment…he would make an <u>ideal husband</u>.

He is a strong noble soul to whom I can feel a companionship so strong and a life so full and happy in his presence that without him it would seem to me now, unendurable. He is…every inch a man, a charming listener, wonderful talker, has traveled constantly spending six years in Europe, is a linguist, well-read, a man of the world but who feels he has not lost <u>all</u> its sweetness. At times he shows a wonderful vim and interest in passing details for a man of thirty-nine.

And then he is so sweet, so tender, so full of gallant thoughts, perfect respect for a good woman though not a lady's man. Well, little journal, I must confess to you the secret heart of my very own heart—I care so much for him that his face, his ideas, his sweet remembrances to me, our happy talks together are forever before me and I realize fully that now having once in my life known the full joy of caring for my superior in every way that I never will marry unless it be him. I would rather die an old maid of seventy than bestow myself on some one for my daily bread and live a life lacking all interest as it needs must be. <u>He has</u> no double and I can never interest myself again.

The Northern Pacific Railroad people on the steamer with whom he was traveling told our friends that he and his father had just sold a mine for several millions—that he was President of a R.R. in Minnesota. I have looked the latter up on the map and from Tower, Minnesota to Duluth seems to me to be a very short distance and whatever it may be in the future it cannot give him so very much now—of course he may be rich but except that he took his colored man traveling with him I saw no indication of wealth or extravagance.

Even if he had only two hundred dollars a month with his bright mind and charming manner I would be perfectly willing to marry him and what is more I make the confession I never even knew before that I could feel I would willingly go into the kitchen to cook for him once a week. That he cares for me there is no doubt but he may try to crush it all out of his life not wishing to marry and so I may never see him again! Oh! The very thought terrified me…I can imagine a cottage however tiny with him would be eternal joy—to travel about and so keep up with his bright mind—simply an ecstatic life.

I feel sorry for Edith, Susie, Bessie and all my friends who have or are to be married and cannot know the joy I feel—with such a partner. I must constantly improve, growing sweeter, happier, and broader in my views from day to day. If I never meet him again I shall wed myself to this past knowing I can love, have loved and will never marry but remain true unto myself. Better a friendship in the past than a future life without love or companionship and there cannot be <u>two</u> souls suiting mine on this small earth.

Nellie and her father continued homeward by train. From Victoria, they traveled overnight to Tacoma, where they spent several days, then on to Portland, Sissons, Redding, and then an overnight train to Oakland on July 3. It is doubtful that Nellie remembered very much of the spectacular scenery of the Cascade Range; her heart was traveling eastward to Duluth with Charlie.

She did not discuss the depth of her feelings with her father, but she did not need to. He knew that she had fallen in love with Charlie Tower. As a devoted father he must have had mixed feelings toward her new suitor—so educated, cultivated, apparently very rich—but a man who would take her to live thousands of miles away.

Frank Smith knew first hand how difficult it was to maintain family ties over great distances, and he recognized the irony in the situation—if Mr. Tower married Nellie and took her to live in the East, it would be no different than when he himself married Susan Rising in New York and took her to live in the West.

5

September or Forever

Nellie had been home for several weeks before she had a chance to write in her diary again and record her pleasure in sharing her happy news with her family.

> How happy I was to be home! I had not intended telling the girls anything about my dear kind friend but I had been so long pent up that to give expressions to my feelings and declare openly my warm friendship for him seemed a privilege. While unpacking with Mama, Cecil, Ada and Gertrude as eager listeners, I told the whole story from the very beginning. It was a real joy to live it all over again. Late in the afternoon, though I had never dreamed I could have done it, the girls begged and so I read them my little journal—they thought it was all so sweet, so pure and so full of happiness. I realized that it was better so, they had always been to me like a part of my own self and if in the following two weeks I had not been able to talk freely of him to them I would have grown grey haired...

By the third week in July, most of the Smith family had dispersed—Nellie's mother, Aunt Sallie and Cecil to the ranch, Ada on a sketching tour and Gertrude visiting friends in Lake Tahoe. Only Nellie and her father remained in the house in Oakland. In the lonely hours, Nellie again turned to her diary:

> Oh! Those ten days on the *Olympian*, journal dear, I lived in another world—a fairyland and with one who has become so dear to me that my life will advance into brilliant sunshine or retreat into densest shadow, according to whether I ever see him again or not..."September or forever" has almost driven me mad at moments. Fortunately he has no idea of the strength of my feeling, so, if we never meet again, he will never know what...I have suffered—this is a real old maid's pride but alas! for our sex it must exist. I feel I could make him so happy and that is saying a great deal when it would mean leaving father, mother, sisters, <u>all.</u>

After I had been home a week the book *John Inglesant*,[1] which he had promised me, and a lovely letter of seven (little) pages arrived—it was so full of sweet thoughts and kind interest in my welfare that I think I must have read it over twenty times, each hour it seems sweeter and dearer to me...

Charlie wrote to Nellie on July 5, shortly after his return to Duluth:

My dear Miss Smith,
    ...It was very hard work for me to go up the street that evening after you had left the dock and had gone out into the stream...I sit here in my own little house and let my mind wander back every day to Alaska...It was a happy time. I never shall forget it. I only wish it were given to us to store up in some way the enjoyment and appreciation of these events in our lives as we go along, instead of having to look back upon them only to value them when they are gone. For instance, I thought those days at Victoria were natural enough, in the course of events; they seemed so at the time; but now it is hard for me to believe that anything so delightful could occur to me in common nature—and I would so gladly live them over again...
Very sincerely, your friend, C. Tower, jr.

Nellie noted in her diary her response to Charlie's letter:

I wrote my dear friend twelve pages and in return asked him when he answered it "to let me know if he was coming to California in September" that, if we were never to meet again I would rather know it now, and <u>force</u> him from my mind than to have to add to the grief and the disappointment of brightest anticipations. Any day this week the answer is due and it makes me so restless I cannot become interested in anything. In my own heart I know I have every reason to expect him but when sometimes I think, suppose he should not come—the blackness of darkest night comes over me and I feel a chill that renders me powerless to act—

In Charlie's next letter from Duluth, written on July 21, 1887, he gave Nellie further cause for anxiety when he explained that his indecision about a trip to California was due in part to "duties and obligations here and elsewhere that can not well be put aside in a moment." Although he said in closing, "I think of you every day," Nellie was thrown into despair. Could Charlie be referring to a previ-

---

1.   *John Inglesant* was a popular novel written by Joseph Henry Shorthouse, published in England in 1880. The story, which concerns twin brothers during the Civil War in England, became popular in the United States.

ous romantic attachment that he would have had to break before he could fully commit himself to her? She wrote Charlie the next day:

Oakland, July 28, 1887
My dear Mr. Tower,
    All day yesterday I felt as though something very good was coming to me—it was explained when your most welcome letter arrived at 4 p.m....
    I enjoyed *John Inglesant* very much....It made me thankful that I did not live in those dim, narrow, dark religious days when sacrament and confession were part of each daily duty...
    When I last wrote you a miserable fear crept into my heart of what we both should lose if we were never to meet again, but now that is all past...
    How often I have wondered at my own bravery the morning you told me that you must leave for Duluth that day. As I readily seconded your going I felt something snap within me but I could pay our friendship no higher compliment than to assist you to "follow principle" and to encourage you to do your "duty."
    I say September for your visiting us but October or even November will be just as favorable for the hunting trip, Lick Observatory, the pine woods of California and the grand new Hotel Del Monte. You shall receive the warmest kind of a welcome whenever you come.
    Farewell my very dear friend. Think of me often
    Yours sincerely, Nellie Smith

Nellie's letter reached Charlie on August 3; his reply was a brief note and a promise to write a proper letter on his return from a trip to the mines. For Nellie, this seemed the longest two weeks of her life.

Finally, on August 15, came the good news: Charlie would definitely make the trip to California:

August 9
My very dear Miss Smith,
    Your letter has given me a great deal of pleasure and I have read it many times since...the days on the *Olympian* were the happiest of my life. There are so many things that I want to say, and so much to hear from you in reply, that writing seems but a poor medium.
    I am amazed that fate brought us together...to that remote country...you from your home and I from so far away and that, almost at the very moment of meeting, each should have recognized in the other something that meant friendship and confidence, and close companionship...Your foresight...was very wonderful to me—nobody else seems to understand my disposition and my purposes, like you. Dearest Friend, I am very happy in the possession of your confidence and friendship. You have mine in return, to the fullest extent

of my feeling…You are not only my Comrade now, you are my hope in a time to come when I know we shall see into each other's eyes again; you are the object of a thousand happy thoughts…

I shall go to you as soon as I can make my arrangements here to leave for a few weeks…

Before leaving for the West, Charlie went to Chicago to meet with Henry Porter and the other members of the syndicate who were purchasing the Duluth and Iron Range Railroad Company and the Minnesota Iron Company. He then went by train to Waterville, New York, to visit his parents in their summer home, and to report to his father on his meetings in Chicago.

Another report which Charlie would have shared with his parents had been hand delivered to him in Duluth on August 9. It was from the private detective whom Charlie had sent to California to investigate the Smith family; the report was most reassuring.

6

E. McDonald, Private Eye

Judging from Nellie's diary, in which she wrote details of her day-to-day life during this anxious period, she had no idea of the existence of E. McDonald, private investigator, of Duluth, Minnesota, who had spent July 18 to 20 making inquiries in San Francisco concerning her father's law practice. Nor was she aware of him during his stay in Oakland, from July 21 to August 1, when he questioned various Oakland residents about her family.

It is hard to believe that it was Charlie's idea to have the Smiths investigated after he had spent a week with both father and daughter on board the *Olympian*. He had seen Nellie in many different situations in which she always comported herself as a well brought up young woman.

Charlie's father, however, had only his lovesick son's word for the integrity of the Smith family. As a new millionaire, the senior Tower may well have needed additional reassurance that the young woman whom his son and heir had met on shipboard was not a fortune hunter.

The senior Charlemagne also may have had reservations about how Nellie Smith, from Oakland California, would fit in with the highly stratified society of the East. The senior Towers considered themselves too elderly to enter into society; when they moved to Philadelphia from Pottsville in 1875, they did little about social position other than buying a substantial home at a good address. Hal Bridges, in his biography of Charlemagne Tower, *Iron Millionaire*, described the Tower home on Spruce Street as "a mansion in the fashionable...district south of Market Street...with eighteen acres of grounds...fruit orchard, hothouse, and gardens."[1]

But Charlemagne knew that his son aspired to a position in the old Philadelphia social hierarchy. Charlie, whose tastes had been refined at Exeter, Harvard and through extensive travel abroad, could easily maintain a position as a prominent member of Philadelphia society if he had the right wife. Although a private

---

1.   Bridges, *Iron Millionaire,* 126.

detective could not be expected to understand the nuances of social position, he could at least report on the Smith's home, their neighborhood, and how they were perceived by their acquaintances.

Blissfully unaware that her family was being scrutinized, the lovesick Nellie continued writing in her journal:

> Sunday Morning—July 31, 1887
>
> My dearest journal I feel so bound up in the blues this morning that I resort to you as a refuge. It is so dark, dreary, and I am so lonesome— I have one comfort—my letter came. I looked all day Monday and Tuesday finally Wednesday it arrived just as I was going to see Mrs. Shelton— it was so sweet, so dear—gave me hope of seeing him again but perhaps not in September. I could wait until Christmas but not longer than that—oh! Sometimes it seems to me since I have been alone that if it were to last much longer I would be insane!
>
> My thoughts will surround him constantly in spite of myself and I feel always so restless, so unequal to exertion, so uncertain as to my future. I make myself busy every moment but oh! how the days drag. Last Wednesday, I received ten letters, his being one—in the morning one came from Mrs. Paul saying she had promised to write me to tell me of Mr. Tower's kind hospitality to them at his pretty home at Duluth when they were obliged to remain over for a whole day to take the Lake Steamer—said they talked after dinner and after supper "of a certain young lady," did my ears burn? That he made a charming host. This letter made me joyous all day and then when his came at 4 p.m. I felt as if I were walking on air.
>
> He wrote that he had told his sister all—from the day that he was wandering through the world alone and came unexpectedly upon a young woman sitting on an anchor and after that our lives flowed on so peacefully together…

The day after Nellie wrote this entry, Detective McDonald completed his investigation and left by train to return to Duluth. In the letter that follows, McDonald summarized his findings, and could barely disguise his enthusiasm. One can imagine him, probably on the West Coast for the first time, surrounded by the beauty of the California summer, hearing nothing but good things about the upstanding Smith family and to have his major informant, the gardener, also named McDonald.

Duluth, 6 August, 1887
Mr. C. Tower Jr.

Dear Sir,

I went to California at your request and stayed there two weeks. I arrived in San Francisco on Monday evening, the 18th July 1887, and stopped at the Palace Hotel until Wednesday evening the 20th July. From the evening of Wednesday, July 20th until Monday afternoon, August 1st, I was at the Galindo Hotel in Oakland. During this period I spent my time between the two places, Oakland and San Francisco, as occasion required.

Mr. G. Frank Smith is a man probably fifty-five years of age. He is of English parentage and was born, I think, in some one of the English Colonies…He studied for the Church, when he was a young man, but abandoned that and he is now a lawyer of excellent standing. His office is at 502 Montgomery Street, in San Francisco, where he goes every morning and returns to Oakland late in the afternoon. His practice is good; it seems to be rather one of consultation than of trying cases in court, and it relates to the business of large corporations or other matters of importance. His office is usually well filled with people. I should think his practice yields him from $10,000 to $12,000 a year. I found that everybody I talked with knew him as a lawyer, generally as a prominent one, and his reputation everywhere is that he is among the foremost in his profession as a counselor, though he is not fluent in trying cases before a jury, and does not appear to have much of that class of business. He is, by general consent, a highly educated man.

He was the leading counsel in the recent trial of the Colton case against C. P. Huntington and the Central Pacific R.R. Co., and I am told the rail road company offered him a salary of $10,000 a year if he would abandon the case, which he declined to do.

He is not a man of great means, though he owns the house he lives in at Oakland. This is worth about $40,000; it is a fine large house with an extensive garden about it. He is especially fond of choice trees and plants, of which the garden contains very many. Some of these have been brought from Japan. The place is exceedingly neat and well kept, as is also everything about the house. There are two horses and two cows in the stable. The servants are Chinese, as is customary in California, except the man who takes care of the horses and the garden, who is an Irishman, named McDonald, born in Boston…

Everything is systematic and is carried on with great neatness and regularity in and about the house. There are electric wires all through the house to light the gas, and wires also leading to two large gas lamps standing in front of the door, one on each side of it; these are in the shape of sphinxes. The house is handsomely furnished throughout.

I found Mr. Smith to be a man who is held in high esteem in the community; I did not meet with anyone at all who said a word against him.…He is not intimate with everybody; I should say he is rather an exclusive man, though his associations are with people who represent the best—not necessarily the richest, but the best educated and the most cultivated. This is true also of the whole family. He is apparently devoted to his profession and gives his whole time to that and to his family. He has no bad habits of any kind, and no irregularities. I call him in every way a good citizen and a good man.

I draw my information chiefly from the Rev. Benjamin Ackley...rector of St. John's Episcopal Church in Oakland and who has known Mr. Smith and his family intimately ever since they came to Oakland; also from J. McDonald, who has lived with Mr. Smith for eight years...Besides these two, I talked with at least a hundred people who knew the family, among these the editors of the Oakland Tribune, the proprietor of the hotel, shopkeepers, business men and others of all classes in the community.

Mr. Smith married a Miss Rising who was born, I think, in Massachusetts, and I believe in Boston. Her father and mother came to Oakland to live; they died there in 1868 and are buried there. One of Mrs. Smith's brothers is a judge in Nevada, I think a United States judge; another brother, now dead, was also a judge, but I do not know where he lived. A sister of Mrs. Smith, Miss Rising, lives with the family in Oakland. Mr. and Mrs. Smith were married before going to California, but I do not know where the marriage took place...

Mrs. Smith is about fifty years of age. She is a splendid woman in every way, in her family and among her friends, and is greatly respected. Mr. Ackley, whose church she attends, spoke of her in the very highest terms. He frequently goes to the house, especially to lunch on Sunday, and he says there could not be a better wife and mother.

There are seven children, four girls and three boys. The oldest is a daughter, married to a Mr. Harvey, a young man of good standing whom I judge to be about thirty-five years of age; he has a ranch in California and is also interested in a mining company...

The next child is a son, Albert; the next is a daughter, Ada; the next is a son, Percy; the next is Nellie; the next Gertrude; the youngest is a son, whose name I do not know, a fine boy but he lost his eye sight from scarlet fever when he was a child, is now about thirteen years of age. None of the children except Mrs. Harvey are married.

The sons are very industrious, and they are talented. Percy has shown decided ability as an electrician, in which connection he is now in Guatemala, in South America. His brother Albert, is with him. They have been there about a year and are doing well. Mr. Ackley spoke especially of the character and industry of these boys; he said they had always earned their own living since they grew up and were unwilling to be dependent upon their father.

The daughters are all accomplished and highly educated. Miss Ada is especially interested in water colour painting, in which she is said to have done some very good work. They are all industrious girls, well brought up by their mother, and each one of them is able to take charge of the household and do her share in its management.

The family entertains a good deal, but usually in a quiet manner and among a class of people who are exclusive, like themselves. The young ladies are very active in the Fruit and Flower Mission, for the relief of the sick and the destitute.

Miss Nellie Smith is a girl of twenty-five or twenty-six, I should say. I saw her twice, picking flowers in the garden; once I was very near to her, but I got no opportunity to speak with her. Mr. Ackley says she is more active in the family and more influential with her father than any of the others. She replaces her mother a great deal in the care of the household and she does much to assist all the others in whatever interests they may have, at home and in society. She is accomplished, is particularly well read and always makes herself interesting in society. Mr. Ackley seemed to prefer her among the members of the family, both as to her character and her general disposition, and says he never knew a better woman. This is confirmed by McDonald, the gardener, who always spoke in praise of Miss Nellie. I talked with very many people about her, each one of whom gave her a kind word; her even temper and her gentle manners have made friends for her everywhere. The impression I have formed of her is that she is an exceptionally good woman in every respect.

This family is very remarkable for the affection that exists between one and another of its members. Mr. Ackley referred to that as something that he has never seen equaled, and McDonald repeatedly told me that he never had heard a harsh word among them in all the time that he has lived there.

I have given great pains and attention to this case, and I have worked it up as thoroughly as I can possibly do. It far surpasses in excellence of result anything I expected to find, and I do not hesitate to say that this is the best family record I have ever found in my whole experience.

E. McDonald

7

Charlie's Visit

Nellie was in rapture when she heard that Charlie would arrive in California in September. After two months of waiting and worrying, vacillating between elation and despair, her mind was at last at ease.

> Sunday, August 28—Well, dear journal, the letter came nearly two weeks ago and brought me with it ecstatic joy!
>
> My precious dear companion is coming to me in September—Oh! The happiness—the ecstasy of seeing him again! In his last letter he wrote that he "recognized the days at Victoria as the happiest of his life"— that he felt pleased to have my "confidence and friendship" and that I possessed his "to the fullest extent of his feeling"—that I was his "companion and comrade"…that after visiting his parents home in New York he was coming out to California to visit me. After reading the letter I jumped about in a wild state of joy…
>
> My trial is waiting—Oh! The days seem so long—I try to interest myself in sketching, sewing and being sociable but I am leading now only a half existence—my full life begins when he arrives in September.
>
> A cot shared with him would be joy and for once in my life I can say, "I love thee so well I could cook for thee three times a day"—this heretofore has been incomprehensible to me. His mind is so bright—we are in such perfect sympathy that life on a desert island would be not only endurable but preferable to life in a king's palace without him.
>
> A trip to the geysers had already been planned for Ada, Gertrude and the Ringstroms—now the idea is that Mr. Tower and I follow in a buggy or if Mr. Forrest can go—then we four in a double carriage—fancy the picture dear journal! The four or five days trip through beautiful woods, stopping at hotels over night and beside me the one companion that I would select in all the whole world! We would have an opportunity most rare to become acquainted and gradually retreat into the unforeseen pages of our past…

Nellie celebrated her twenty-ninth birthday on September 2, 1887. This year, her future looked a good deal brighter to her than it had the year before. Her mother's birthday letter was filled with portent of things to come:

> …The coming year may be a very important one in your life—and filled with happiness, or it may be embittered with sorrow, and disappointment. In either case, my <u>Nellie</u> will be strong, with God's help, to go forth, and fight the battle for life nobly—
>
> Oh Darling I cannot tell you all I wish and hope for you. That my Love could shield you from <u>all</u> harm, but that you may be kept from evil, and be prepared for the life beyond, is the constant desire of
> Your devoted Mother

Recording the day's events in her diary, Nellie was fairly bursting with excitement:

> September 2, 1887
> What a happy day this has been to me my darling journal—long will I remember the hungry expectance of yesterday and my happiness today when his letter came this afternoon…
> This evening I talked with Papa freely of our friendship and Papa said after some reflection, "how can we ever give you up?" I said, "Oh, you will all come and live in Duluth." I was so happy to have the chance of talking so seriously to Papa and now he knows I love Mr. Tower but he can never fathom <u>how</u> much.
> Sept. 19, in the green room 8:40 pm
> I am so happy tonight, dear journal. I expect my dear lovely man one week from tomorrow night—how can I <u>ever</u> wait! His photo arrived today and although not flattering it is excellent and makes me so happy I have not wanted it out of my sight. It is three months this Thursday since we parted and how interminable they have been!
> Can it be really me who is to have so much joy—a life in a tiny cot would be happy with him and when I think that besides we may travel—that we can keep up in all the new magazines and pictorial papers—that I may leave this much disliked Oakland—that I may give many pleasures to others—my heart beats ecstatically! As I look into his eyes now I realize that he is the love of my whole life and if I never had seen him again my happy hours would belong to the past. To think that he must feel he cannot live without me is the greatest joy that can come into my life…
> I hope Duluth may be our home for a while to put life into his lovely home there and spend a few quiet months there first with him would be to me ideal!
> Sunday Evening—Sept. 25, l887

I cannot realize that this time tomorrow night he will be here! Papa will call upon him and escort him over on the 4:30 pm. boat. With what an agitated heart I will await the arrival of that train and when I again really shake his hand and look into his eyes I will be in ecstasy.

This coming Wednesday we all start for the Geysers—could anything be more ideal? Perfect moonlight nights resting at hotels at night—driving together through the day—we had all sorts of little experiences—oh! Those happy, happy hours before me!

We have made changes in our drawing room and tomorrow have so many little delicious finishing touches to put around the house—life starts anew for me tomorrow—he has come to me. My whole life must be joyous if it be spent with him—how lovely the dear ones have all been to me during my long trial.

On September 14, the day before he left Duluth, Charlie wrote to his father describing the final plans for the Minnesota Iron Company and Railroad under the new ownership.

Richard Henry Lee, married to Charlie's sister, Deborah, who had worked with Charlie on the Minnesota project throughout, would be vice president of the Iron Range Railroad and he, Charlie, would be a member of the five man executive committee which would oversee both companies. Charlie would return to Philadelphia, and travel to New York, or Duluth, or Chicago as required. Charlie wrote his father : "I feel that I am going into a wider field by an association as close as this with these men than if I should stay here in the management as I have been before. They are in front rank among business men, their interests are large and diversified, and their ability is certainly of a high order...I can not escape a feeling of sadness at the breaking up of my association here; but I would not change it now if I could; I have much hope and confidence in the time to come."

Charlie's visit was, if possible, even more sublime than Nellie had anticipated. After he left, she recalled his visit in her diary:

Mr. Tower arrived September 26 as I expected and remained seventeen days; we drove in three carriages to the Geysers—Gertrude, the Ringstroms, Ada, Mr. Forrest, Flo and LeRoy, Mr. Tower and I in our own carriage. Long days we sat together side by side.

We reached the Geysers at 8pm of a gorgeous moonlight night and then—Ah! My one regret of our whole friendship—but let me forget that stolen kiss if possible...

The afternoon we spent on the creek, Mr. Tower and I a little apart—Oh! How little progress we made in talking hours together for we had all our past, present and future to discuss and going home time came only too soon. Sunday afternoon we started to drive to Healdsburg—did not reach there until 12 am, so there we were riding for ten hours resting only for dinner and what a moonlight night it was!

The next day we drove from Healdsburg to Sonoma and that was one of the happiest days in my life. He had told me the night before that he loved me and that he never could live without me—so this day we planned a future life together. Our tastes seemed to interweave like the figures on a Persian carpet, but all luxuries seemed like mere dross in comparison to the sweetness of the life itself with the one man in all the wide world for me.

Returning home from Sonoma we spent the next eight days going to the city to look about, drove to the Cliff House, two days in Oakland, an afternoon with Meg, a dinner with Floie, another with Mrs. Colton—an evening at the theatre, then a delightful visit to the Chinese quarters—Mr. Tower went duck hunting one night with Papa, and he had a lovely day at Sausalito with Aunt Sallie. We were always chaperoned—twice we went into the Fair and sat down to listen to the music—happy souls were we! I believe that happily married couples are right and that we shall only begin to <u>live</u> when our life commences together…

How many times the dear man hugged me to his heart and tried to kiss me—said I was "only a little girl but caused such a big feeling" and "oh! I love you." My whole soul went out to him—I longed to lavish my love upon him—but he was free and we were not engaged. I knew he cared more for me than even I had ever dreamed of, but it was his wish and he must be right. I promised to protect and shield him and wait patiently until I heard his plans. Sometimes I kissed my darling, may God forgive me if it was wrong, but in the few times I yielded to the many temptations it was storing up his wonderful love to comfort me in these days of loneliness that must follow.

I confessed to Mama and Papa that I had kissed him and then Mr. Tower and I had a lovely talk with Mama—they were all pleased with him—my heart ached with longing to better understand why we were not engaged while he was here—but he asked me to trust him…That dreadful hour of parting again had to come, but it only meant a speedier reunion. We parted on Wednesday, Oct. 12.

Charlie had good reason to delay making his formal proposal to Nellie. At the time of his California to visit he still lived in Duluth and did not know until just before he left for the West that he would, after all, be moving to Philadelphia.

He had no home in Philadelphia, other than his parents' house or the Union League Club where he would stay for a few days at a time. He had been away from the city for over five years; he needed time to move back, look for a suitable house, and renew old friendships.

As becomes clear in his letters written to Nellie during late November and December, he was quite overwhelmed by the responsibility of caring for another person, one whom he loved so much. Because Nellie was ten years younger than he and had led a sheltered life, Charlie had an almost paternal desire that everything be perfect for her.

Only when everything was ready in Philadelphia would he write to Nellie's father requesting her hand in marriage. Then, on receipt of her father's letter to him agreeing to the marriage, he would send Nellie the engagement ring. These were the formalities that were observed in polite society.

Nellie could look past his almost fussy concerns and see Charlie for what he was for her—a gallant protector and provider, the very ideal of a perfect Victorian husband.

8

Will the Letter Ever Come?

In her short but intense relationship with Charlie thus far, Nellie had learned to wait, sometimes patiently, sometimes not so patiently. Now she had the most interminable wait of all—for Charlie's formal proposal.

Until she was officially betrothed, she could not talk about Charlie or their future plans except to her family and a few close friends. This was agony for her. She wanted to have everyone share her happiness.

To make the time go faster, she visited her friend Annie Cope in the hills above Oakland, to take a rest and so divert her mind during the necessitated period of waiting. "It was a wise move," she noted in her diary:

> I so entered into her interests I forgot myself and then later in the joy of telling her I lived in my new love again. We enjoyed lovely October days together reading aloud from *Anna Karennina* and watching the beautiful phases of Mount Diablo—I remained ten days, and also visited the Cook ranch so beloved by Mrs. Colton.

When she returned home from Annie's she found a letter from Charlie written on the train and mailed from Chicago on October 17:

> My dear Miss Nellie,
>   I have been constantly talking to you during the five days and nights that I have spent on the train…I look back with gratitude to the great kindness of all of your family; that I shall appreciate as long as I live.
>   To you, my dear little girl, I look as to a picture of loveliness and gentleness throughout a time that I know was trying to you…no woman could have gone through it more nobly…
> Good Bye—
> May everything good always be with you—
> Your affectionate Friend,
> C. Tower, junior

A week later Nellie received Charlie's second letter, mailed from Duluth on October 23:

> My dear Miss Nellie,
>   I have had so much time to reflect and plan, in the silence of the week that followed when I left you, that my mind is full to overflowing. My one object is to do for you all that I can to fill your life with happiness; so far as a man may do this for a woman my mind and heart are bound to you in devotion and constant endeavor...
>   I shall go to Philadelphia in about a week...the family will then have returned to town from Waterville for the winter...
>   Goodbye dear heart, I have not said even a small part of the things I have in mind to say...Believe that I am yours
>   Faithfully and affectionately,
>   C. Tower, junior

On October 31, Nellie visited another close friend in whom she could confide. She recorded the visit in her diary:

> I went to visit Ella Plummer and had a beautiful visit. It is a grand spot and we spent hours and hours by the ever-changing restless sea. A November storm brought in great high tossing waves and Ella and I lolled in the white sand, walked in the high bluffs, examined the coves, drove through the redwoods with her ever kind husband—gazed in silent admiration at the beautiful waterfall, read Richelieu aloud and talked of my sweet happy life to come. I was ecstatic in my joy—I felt so well, so happy, so glad to be alive and everything sang out to me in the Spring all waiting ends and a new life begins!

When she returned on November 17, she still had not received the letter of proposal from Charlie, but ten days later, it came. Charlie's style was at times ponderous but always heartfelt. The length and detail of the letter give a good indication of the extent of his planning:

> Philadelphia
> 21 November, 1887
> My dearest Nellie,
>   It has been the single object of my thought in the time since I left you, to select a course out of the ways that have been open to me that should prove the one to do the most good for you and ultimately to bring the greatest happiness into your life. I do not know that I shall ever be able to explain to you how much I felt this to be a grave responsibility, or how deeply anxious it has made me. I never realized before how seriously a man looks into the world to

consider all its thousand turns and chances as he must do when he comes to think of the welfare of another besides himself whom he loves better than himself...

This however, I am sure of—that I look with hope and I see good promise, because I have every confidence in the world in you, I love you and honor you above all women and I am ready to devote my life to care for you, to defend you and to give you joy...

Since coming home, I have done much in the way of making plans; let me tell you what I propose.

In the first place, if you come to Philadelphia as a stranger I want you to have every advantage that I can control in obtaining your position here. Therefore, I intend to have a house ready, all but the furnishing of it which I want you to do, so that you may get into it in time to send out your cards and hold your receptions before the present season ends.

I consider this of great importance and I trust you will be able to make your arrangements so as to help me in carrying it out.

People leave the City quite early in the spring; at all events, the Season is pretty well over by the first of May, so that whatever we wish to do must be done before that time. My idea is, to have your receptions in April—If we miss that, they would have to go over until a year from now, when the new Season is just commencing; and in that event very considerable advantage would be lost, which it might take years perhaps to make up for.

You intimated that you should not require more than about two months in which to get ready to be married. Will you not please name some time in January?...

Then we should have an opportunity to go to Santa Barbara for a couple of weeks and to come to Philadelphia in February. You would have time to furnish your house, which I presume would take at least a month, and yet be ready to make your entrance in April.

I take it for granted that you will not care to be seen here much before you have sent out your cards for your receptions, and I shall arrange as it may best please you, either to stay very quietly in Philadelphia or to spend the interim, or most of it, in New York.

We may remain here during April and May, for at that season the city is very agreeable. After that we shall still have the house in Duluth where we may go for the summer, or take the alternative which will be much more attractive I think, to go to Europe for a few months, if my Fathers health will permit me to be absent.

If we are obliged to content ourselves with Duluth, then I think we should find it pleasant to go to Boston in June and be at the Call Day, and Commencement of Harvard University before setting out for the West...

I have one house in view that offers a good deal of what I want, comfortable arrangement and good locality; you know the latter plays an important part in Philadelphia life and I intend to start as well in these matters as I can by any means provided.

I went to Waterville last week to look at a pair of horses that my Uncle Reuben got for me. I like them very much and I think you will when you see them. They are dark bay, sixteen hands high thoroughbreds, and they came from Kentucky. I hope we shall have many a drive to the Park such as we talked about in the lovely days when we were driving through Sonoma.

There are many other details that I am thinking of, but I shall tell you them later, when we have an opportunity to talk them all over. You know I think of you all of the time and I am constantly imagining something that I should like to do for you. Tomorrow I shall write a letter to your Father, which will probably arrive a day later than this—After I have received his reply, and yours, I shall send you the ring and the photographs as you asked me to do. I wish you would please send me something to show the size of your finger so that I may have the ring made to fit exactly. I shall have it measured here at once and shall send it as soon as possible afterwards.

I wait anxiously to hear from you, my Darling, and still more so, a thousand more, to see you and be with you again. After the next meeting, we need never part, and in that thought are wrapt up all the happiness, all the hope and all the joy that I can picture to myself in life.

My family is deeply interested in you. My Father and Mother and sisters stand ready to welcome you and take you into their hearts. My Uncle Reuben makes me tell him about you always when I am with him. The dear old man has grown so fond of you that I do not think he realizes that he has never seen you.

Good Bye—God bless you—
Your devoted and affectionate,
C. Tower Junior

9

Betrothal 1887

Nellie received the long awaited letter from Charlie on November 28, 1887. They had known each other for only six months, a remarkably short acquaintance for that time. Nellie wrote Charlie on November 29 and accepted his proposal:

> My very dear Friend,
>
> With mingled feelings of great joy and sorrow I reread your lovely letter received yesterday morning. "Great joy" that you love me and want to take me before the whole world as your wife!
>
> My heart goes out to you in deepest admiration and warmest love—when you have read this letter you will be mine. I will be yours—we will be as one—a few months more and then arm in arm we can climb the hill of life together—I hope to be your sunlight and you to me...I cannot possibly prepare to leave home before Feb. 8th or 9th.
>
> I am delighted with all your plans. I am sure the house will exactly suit me and it will be a great pleasure for me to furnish it with you. Will we not have a merry time shopping together as we had those happy mornings in Victoria?
>
> Think of driving to Fairmount Park with <u>you</u>! The receptions will be charming—yes, you are right they should be given this season. I consent to that when I say I will be married to you Feb.8th or 9th. I had never dreamed that in my life I could really feel happiness in leaving all the world behind me to share it with <u>one</u> other; the choice has been given me and with you—a whole lifetime with <u>you</u> gives me a strange delight. I love all the world better for knowing you and can give those whom I care for no better wish than that some day they may love another as I love you...
>
> The enclosed ring is the exact size of my finger—let me hear from you every day—if only a line...For today goodbye—my very dear friend,
>
> <u>Yours ever</u>, Nellie

Charlie had written a few days earlier to Nellie's father, requesting her hand in marriage. Frank Smith wrote Charlie on November 29 giving his consent:

I am in receipt of your favor, wherein you ask for the hand of my daughter Nellie. Of course I expected this, and was not unprepared for the proposal, but it is hard to say "yes", and yet I am satisfied that my consent should follow the direction of her own affection.

In all candor, I wish that it had been otherwise, and that her choice had been nearer home, so that the consummation of her happiness would not necessarily have curtailed ours...

Nellie recorded the details of the wedding plans in her diary:

The wedding will take place in the morning—I will have ten maids of honor and about one hundred of my most intimate friends about me to wish me joy on my happiest of days...

The dear darling man wishes to take me to Santa Barbara for two weeks—then to Philadelphia. The month of March we will furnish the house—fancy little me walking into stores with my beloved purchasing *ad libertum* beautiful curtains, pictures, china, cut glass etc. We will be part of that time in New York—during April and May we will keep house—Oh! What joy with <u>him</u>! Then in June, he proposes that we go to Europe for a few months if his father's health permits. If not, then to Duluth—my dear Duluth—where he has spent lovely hours thinking of me and wishing for me and my heart yearning for him...

Each member of my family has shed a few tears over my leaving them, as I have myself...

Charlie pursued his quest for the perfect house for Nellie. On November 28 he gave Nellie a progress report:

Philadelphia,
My dearest Nellie,
I have ransacked the city for a house to live in...I think I have succeeded at last in discovering one that you will like, on the East side of Rittenhouse Square, in 18th Street a little way north of Spruce. It is brick, three stories high, rather old fashioned but highly respectable, with very great advantage of situation...I have had plumbers and builders examining it during the last few days...

I have got you a very handsome brougham, and I intend to have it ready, with horses, harness and coachman, for you to use immediately upon your arrival in Philadelphia...

I do not believe you can understand the anxiety that I have about it all. You are so far away that I cannot consult you as I should so like to do, and yet I must act...As it is, I shall reserve everything for you to decide upon that can be postponed until after your arrival.

Goodbye, I send you my love,
Your affectionate CT. jr.

When Charlie next wrote to Nellie, on Dec. 2, he had decided to lease the house on Rittenhouse Square:

Philadelphia
My dearest Nellie,
I have taken the house in Rittenhouse Square that I wrote you about, and the workmen are in it already making the changes and repairs that are necessary. They promise to get through before the middle of January, which I am anxious to have them do, and I am using all the force I can to accomplish it...The house belongs to an Estate and can not be bought, but I have a Lease for five years, which can be extended at the end of the term, almost indefinitely; for tenants are not likely to be disturbed as long as they wish to stay there. I could not find a house for sale that I considered entirely suitable...

I have a handsome pair of diamond earrings for you, which I shall bring with me when I come. I got them at Caldwell's a few weeks ago, and I hope you will like them. In the meantime, I am not quite sure that your ears are pierced; I do not remember seeing you wear earrings—if they are not, will you not please have them pierced before I come?

It strikes me that my letters to you have become very business-like, of late, with all the propositions that I have to offer, but you see it can not well be otherwise, for I am constantly thinking of you and there are so many things I want to do for you...

In addition to finding a suitable house, Charlie was busy renewing acquaintances in Philadelphia:

Philadelphia
My dearest Nellie,
...I have taken immense pains to revive my associations here among the people whom I want you to know and like and whom I want to like you...I am anxious for you to be happy in your new home and in the associations that you will find here—I would not leave a stone unturned where I thought I could help you in this.

Our engagement has now been formally announced. I wrote several letters, as I told you I should, and mailed them all at once. The news has been received very kindly; already I have many replies, and many good words are said by people whom I meet....

I have been very much perplexed during the last few days, however, by an incident that has occurred most unexpectedly to me...It is an offer made to me of a very important position in a Banking House here, quite unsolicited and unknown to me until I was sent for and received the proposition...

I have never thought of going into financial matters; I should have preferred a Railroad. But this is a very remarkable opportunity; it will place me at once in the front rank of business men in Pennsylvania; it is accompanied by great responsibility, and it may lead to almost anything...

I never knew such an offer made to a man of my age—

My acceptance would...prevent us from leaving Philadelphia next summer. I should take a house in the country near enough to come to town every day and in that way we should escape the city in hot weather. I shall write you more about it later on.

I wish you would write to me often—whenever you feel like it and do not wait to reply to my letters. It always gives me joy to hear from you. I shall be looking for a letter in a day or two telling me about the arrival of your ring. I hope you like it.

Good Bye

Your ever loving CT Jr.

When he received Frank Smith's letter giving his consent to the marriage, Charlie sent Nellie the engagement ring, a large sapphire with two diamonds on either side.

December 21

Philadelphia

My darling Nellie,

...I am very happy to know that the ring fits your hand exactly...

The time drags with me every day, for I am so impatient to be with you....The house is coming along finely, so that I think I shall get it done as far as I expected before I leave for California. Yes, there will be an excellent room for our <u>own</u> sitting room, and you shall furnish it just as you like. I want it to be really the most <u>comfortable</u> room in the house. I can tell you all about this when I see you. You know it will only be about a month now before I start to go to you. How happy I shall be to have you by me once more!

We have been in hopes that some of my sisters could go with me to the wedding, and possibly we may arrange it yet, though there are difficulties in the way, by reason of the long distance. If Dick Lee can leave his post long enough I will take a railroad car and make up a small party, including Emma,

Deborah, possibly Ettie, "old Beck" and Uncle Reuben. They are exceedingly anxious to go, and we are discussing the subject every day; but unless I can carry it out as I intend, I think it would be better to give up the idea and go alone. We shall see.

I want to remind you of our conversation about your dresses. I know it is rather a delicate matter...Do not get anything beyond what you need until we get to New York. I intend to go there directly from Chicago on our way to the East, and not to come to Philadelphia until we have had a day or two to rest from the journey. I have arranged for a suite of rooms at the Buckingham Hotel (which is now the nicest place in New York), where I hope we shall be able to stay for a couple of weeks at least, coming back and forth to Philadelphia as occasion may require us to do in the furnishing of our house. In the meantime, while you are in New York you can do whatever you like in the way of dressmakers.

I am still considering the subject of the Bank, about which I wrote you—and very seriously—I believe I shall accept the place finally. I must give my answer within a week.

I shall write you again tomorrow or the next day—Write to me often, will you not?

Your ever loving
C.T.jr.

From Nellie's Diary, Christmas Day:

My sapphire and diamond ring is glittering on my finger thus indicating the joy that has come into my life this year. Next Christmas I will decorate my own fireside with my darling lover and husband. We three girls and Mama went over to Mrs. Colton's last night to a Christmas festivity and the whole house was like a beautiful dream of gaslight and flowers. Tomorrow night we have our tree and such fun! Today I have answered letters of welcome from Mrs. Tower and two of his sisters—oh! My darling—soon our lives will be interwoven—seven weeks and we will be man and wife—what perfection of happiness life with that blessed!

Nellie wrote to Charlie, December 27 in a state of euphoria:

Oakland
My precious dear,

Your welcome telegram arrived yesterday morning and gave me a thrill of delight; half an hour later your letter came and then I felt very happy once again. You do write beautifully sweetheart and your letters <u>fill</u> one with joy....But oh! When once again we are together—when I can hear your rich voice call and say "Oh! Yes, I do—awfully"— Oh! The delight of the days we have been together!...

Last night we had a tree in our drawing room after dining at Mrs. Harvey's. Your photograph was placed opposite me and beside my absent brothers embedded in ferns and Christmas red berries...I received many lovely presents and one that I prize particularly was a <u>large</u> watercolor of the Santa Barbara Mission that we may have framed for our drawing-room. This was by particular request and much entreaty to Sister Ada knowing how much you too would prize it.

Now about your business plans. I am very proud that you had such an opportunity offered you and in my letter which I will receive next Thursday morning from you it will state your decision...

The disarrangement of our summer plans is a very small matter...Duluth has had every possible charm for me and that would be my only disappointment with the change of programming...Europe does not begin to charm me for three months this summer as the prospect of that quiet lovely spot for me to retreat to with my very own and there to enjoy the rapture of my undisturbed days together in the spot of land where he worked his way and crowned himself with honors.

I told you when we were together that I wanted you to live an active business life—the world would hold with its daily routine greater interest for you then...

Your devoted betrothed—Nellie

On December 29 Charlie reported on his decision about the position at the bank:

My darling Nellie,
...I have accepted the position in the Bank, and I shall write you the details of it very soon. It is the Vice-Presidency of a large finance company of which Mr. Wharton Barker is President and it is considered by all my advisors as a great opportunity for me. I shall have to begin with my new duties next Tuesday...

Good Bye, with all my love,
Your devoted CTjr

Charlie was impatient to get the house finished before he left Philadelphia to go to California in February, but the work had slowed down during the Christmas holidays. He wrote Nellie on December 30:

Philadelphia

My darling Nellie,

I have spent nearly all day today consulting about the work that remains yet to be done on our house before I leave here to go to you—Time is crowding me with all the little details of it, and since I shall be obliged to spend every day at the Bank from ten o'clock until three, after next Monday, I shall be rather less able to look after it myself. But it will come out all right, I think.

In view of the fact that time is now an element to be considered, I [will] send to Mr. Louis Tiffany, of New York, a well known decorator in this part of the world, and get him to carry out my ideas and to suggest corrections in them where he saw fit. It is with one of his men that I have spent the day; he came over this morning and went home at nightfall...My idea in getting Tiffany now is, that the painting and papering may be done under his supervision, and then later on when we come to New York and are buying our furniture, he will tell us where to go and will help us to shop if we want him.

There is a large, long parlor, with two windows upon Rittenhouse Square and two at the back end, two doors leading into it from the hallway, a fire place in the centre of the wall opposite the doors, and the ceiling is fourteen feet high. I think I shall make this a light blue, with a handsome colonial mantelpiece, painted white, and light tiles above the fireplace.

The dining room is 27 feet long by 15 feet, with three windows one side (South), one large square window with plate glass at the East end, and an open fireplace. I think of making this a deep red, with lighter cherry or mahogany mantel, and tiles to accord.

There are two fine bathrooms, entirely new and fresh. I shall have the walls lined with small white tiles (like little white bricks), four feet from the floor all around, and above them, have it tinted to make it look bright and pretty, and on the floors you will perhaps decide to have some warm colored carpet or handsome rugs made to fit. One of these bathrooms leads out from the bedroom, with a door between, and each has a large window.

There are two handsome rooms on the second story, connected by a door, the front one looking out onto the square, with three windows; each of these has also an open fireplace. The back room will be the bedroom and the front one shall be our own absolutely private sitting room, comfortable, bright, attractive, and with you in it, lovely. The bedroom will be pink; the front room will correspond in some way but will not be quite as light as the other, and it will have a pretty mantelpiece and tiles...

I do not think I shall do much with the spare rooms, of which there are two and another large room that may be a library and sitting room, upstairs, until you come. I am undecided about that, though I think I shall have the necessary painting done in them and the walls prepared, even if I do not paper them.

You see you are with me in every thought of my daily life. Oh for the time when you will be with me indeed! I long for you, you sweet little girl...

Good Bye, my dear one,
Your devoted CTJr.

10

Together Forever, 1888

Nellie was blissfully happy as she greeted the New Year. She was in love. In five short weeks she would marry Charlemagne Tower Junior, whom she considered the most wonderful man in the world. Only occasionally did she wonder if she was living a happy dream that might soon come to an end.

At times—when she least expected it—she felt a great sadness at the thought of leaving her family She knew that her parents dreaded her departure. Her mother kept busy every moment, reviewing details for the wedding reception and working with Nellie and her sisters sewing items for the trousseau. Nellie's father worked longer than usual hours at his law office; at home, he maintained an attitude of forced cheerfulness.

Nellie's first letter in the New Year, written on January 1, 1888, was to her beloved Charlie:

Oakland
Happy New Year my precious sweetheart!…

I have arranged a unique little program which will enable my dearest friend to await us at the altar; my two unmarried sisters only acting as bridesmaids and preceding me in the wedding march. If your sister will be persuaded to come I will also ask my most intimate friend and then we will have four bridesmaids.

In the evening I sent another telegram to use the name "Helen" if possible. We all feel this would be a favorable opportunity for me to adopt a more formal name to use in the future signing my name on ceremonious occasions or for extremely formal notes. The dictionary gives Nellie as an abbreviation of Helen, therefore, I feel perfectly honest in doing so. I will always be "Nellie" to you, to my family and dear friends, otherwise Helen.

It never occurred to me until you suggested it and then the more I thought of it the more necessary it seemed to me for future formalities. When I am old, very old, Nellie will be inappropriate—won't it sweetheart?

Nellie continued to record the details of her days in her diary:

> What changes this New Year is to bring and oh! How happy I am. My letters
> from my sweetheart are so satisfactory—he begins to so long for me that he
> writes me it is hard for him to "remain there his allotted time" it is better
> so—our engagement is so short and now I can spend every moment with my
> dear ones. I simply do not realize in the least all the joy and ecstasy that await
> me...
>
> Two of my dresses are being made in New York at Mrs. Colton's dress-
> maker and my wedding dress at Mrs. Switzer's and my tea gowns and under-
> clothes at home. The girls are helping me and we have such dear cozy times
> sewing—we plan the lovely times we will have when they visit me in Philadel-
> phia.
>
> My darling has found a house opposite Rittenhouse Square thinking that
> with open space about me I would feel less confined—was not that dear of
> him? He has a carriage and horses and diamond earrings for me but these are
> all as nothing beside his love his grand character which all my family thor-
> oughly admire—his dear ones and friends have written me letters of welcome
> and he has left no stone unturned for my future happiness.

Charlie was inexhaustible in his planning for Nellie's future happiness, and
safety. When he wanted to buy a well-trained pair of driving horses that could be
trusted to remain steady both in city traffic and on country lanes, he turned to his
bachelor uncle Reuben Tower, a noted horseman, who lived in Waterville, New
York. Reuben decided on a matched pair of bay geldings that Charlie had first
seen when he visited his parents at their summer home before he went to California. As soon as he settled on the house on Rittenhouse Square, Reuben shipped
the horses to Philadelphia by train. Charlie reported to Nellie on January 5:

> Philadelphia
> My Nellie Darling,
>   ...Uncle Reuben sent me my horses a few weeks ago, because I wanted to
> get used to them and have them get used to the sights and sounds of the city
> before I go away. They are the nicest pair I ever drove. I have only used them
> in the buggy as yet, but even then I can not help wishing for you every time I
> go out and anticipating the delight of having you by me—if the time will only
> hurry and bring me to you. I have an excellent English coachman, who has
> been with the horses three years, and in whom I have all the more confidence
> for that. I do not intend to take any risk with the dearest and sweetest little
> woman in all of the world.

I am afraid we shall not get up the party to go to California, though it is still being talked of. There are a great many difficulties in the way of so long a journey in mid-winter when there are several people to look after.
Good Bye my beloved,
Your devoted C. T. jr.

On the same day, Nellie wrote to Charlie:

Oakland
My own precious dear,
What a sweet dream I had about you last night—you were here with me and we were so happy, "together forever" we said…
I would like to have low sweet music play the Wedding March for us—"Call Me Thine Own" during the ceremony and "Lohengrin's Wedding March" afterwards. Does this accord with your idea? The musicians will probably include a violinist, cellist, pianist and lutist who will all be positioned in the small court of the front hall between the stairs and the hat rack. Have you any suggestions to make?
Your devoted sweetheart,
Nellie

In Charlie's next letter to Nellie, written on January 7, he again mentioned Nellie's use of the name Helen on formal occasions after they were married. As the wedding drew near, the name change would become more of an issue, especially with Nellie's parents.

Philadelphia
My darling Nellie,
After your letter of the 30th came yesterday, I was again inclined to use the name Helen in the invitations, so I telegraphed you this morning to ask you finally if you still prefer it. I like it exceedingly myself, and if it is not distasteful to your Father and Mother, let us decide upon that for all the cards…
I modified the first plan for the house somewhat and I am now entirely satisfied. The prettiest and most attractive of all will be the bedroom and our private sitting room adjoining it. These you are sure to like. I am so glad to have one of Miss Ada's watercolors; it will be very beautiful to hang in the drawing room.
Good Bye my best beloved,
Your devoted CT jr.

A staff of servants would be needed in the Rittenhouse Square house. Charlie told Nellie in his letter of January 10 that he had already hired two of the people they would need:

Philadelphia
My Nellie Darling,

The man who is going to California with me, and who will travel with us is an English trained servant. I think he will do for the dining room when we get back; he is very capable. The coachman I have also, as I told you in one of my letters, an Englishman as well.

I am undecided about the house in Duluth, whether to keep it going until next summer with the hope that you and I may spend even a week there together, or whether to close it now. I want you very much to be with me and live with me a few days in the place where I spent the years of my life immediately before we came together, where I first wrote to you and where I thought and dreamed about you until you entered into and became a part of my existence…

In one month from today you will be mine. Shall you be happy, my dear one? I am sure it will be to me the greatest happiness I have ever known.
Good Bye—I love you well
Your affectionate CT jr.

By January 18, Charlie was just as excited as Nellie that they would soon be together:

Philadelphia
My darling little Nell,

One week from today I leave Philadelphia to go to you. How happy we shall be my Darling, when we are together again…Three weeks from today will be our wedding day. You are thinking the same thing now, are you not? But I count the beginning of my joy even earlier than that—from the time of my meeting you, for then we shall never have to part again as we have done.

I shall only write once or twice more, because I hope to see you on Monday (the 30th) and letters sent at the end of this week will scarcely get there before me. But I shall telegraph you, as I said.

The change of name to Helen has indeed assumed considerable importance for so small a matter. After all, I was afraid your Father and Mother might feel just as it appears they do feel about it—And it was with that in view that I concluded to have the announcement cards made in San Francisco. Is it not best, as it has turned out, my dear one?
Good Bye my well beloved,
    Your own, C.T.jr.

Thanks to Charlie's many letters, Nellie was able to follow the renovation of the house on Rittenhouse Square almost as closely as if she were in Philadelphia instead of three thousand miles away in Oakland. From Charlie's January 20 letter, the last he would address to her as "Miss Nellie Smith":

> My Nellie Darling,
> I have written a letter to your Mother that will go in the same mail with this, rather late…
> I have got from New York a full set of the samples of decorations in our house, the halls and rooms, each by itself, to show you the colors and the combinations. These I shall bring with me to California, so that you may look at them as soon as possible, for no doubt you are curious to see what sort of hand I have made of it in house decoration.
> The painters have begun now, and I have very good promise that they will be through by the first of March, or, at all events, so nearly through that when you see the house it will be presentable and ready also for you to choose your furniture.
> This is the last time I shall write to you before I start for California, because this letter will probably not reach you before Saturday, and, if all goes well, I hope to see you on Monday.
> Good Bye, my own dear one,
> Your devoted, CT.jr.

From Nellie's diary:

> Sunday night—Jan 22, 1888
> My darling journal—how happy I am! My dearly beloved leaves for California on Wednesday next and in one week more it will seem like the beginning of the end. The hardest part of my trousseau is finished now—the lovely tea gowns are exquisite, the underclothes with their dainty ribbons and laces are to be laid away in their boxes—my trunk has arrived—the wedding dress, made at Mrs. Switzer's, comes tomorrow—my travelling dress also from the East—now only remains to be done last errands and a few stitches here and there.
> I do not even now realize that I am so soon to leave my home forever—we all live in my happiness and will not think of the separation that comes in the near future. His letters are so dear and oh! I am so happy.

Nellie wrote a final diary entry before Charlie arrived:

Sunday Evening Jan. 29, 1888

My darling journal—if all goes well my sweetheart will be with me tomorrow night—I have received telegraphs from him every day and he is so far safe and making good time—my trousseau is about completed and everything so lovely—Mr. Tower's family have sent in all their presents—solid silver tea set, forks and spoons—Oh! It is all so lovely—after he arrives I will begin more to realize my departure [from her family] which now seems not a part of it. We all refuse to see any but the bright side and are contemplating with greatest pleasure the wedding day. All my friends and acquaintances are so lovely and say to me such beautiful things that I feel myself very happy and proud.

Mr. Tower wrote Mama a beautiful letter bidding them all welcome to our new home—Oh! My darling—how much we have to talk over, and now my full life is just commencing. Am I not the most fortunate girl to be going to lead such an ideal life with the love of my heart. Oh! My treasure— this time tomorrow oh! yes, my own.

In the end, no one from Charlie's family was able to attend the wedding. The long train trip across the Rocky Mountains in the middle of winter was difficult, and could be dangerous.

Charlie's father and mother and his Aunt Henrietta Page sent a telegram, "May brightness and blessings be with Mr. and Mrs. Charlemagne Tower Jr. today and always."

George H. Ellsbury, of Tower City, Dakota Territory, an old friend of Charlie's with whom he had worked in Duluth, wrote the following tribute to be read as a wedding toast.

To My friend—
Chimes are ringing in the West,
Happy Day! May it be blest,
And may its echo, loud and clear,
Reach kindred hearts both far and near.
Lo! On a distant shore this day,
Even over the mountains far away,
My boy has gone to claim a wife,
And take a partner for this life.
God! Open wide the "Golden Gate"!
Now give my son a loving mate.
Each vow here taken, may they keep
Through future life, and may they reap
Of health, of wealth, of joy and love,
Which are rich blessings from above,
Each have abundance, some to spare,
Remember this a mother's prayer.

Just Hark! I hear, at home they say,
Return, as one, and with us stay.

G. H. Ellsbury, February 8, 1888

From the *Oakland Inquirer,* Feb. 8, l888:

MARRIED AT MID-DAY

The Tower-Smith Nuptials Celebrated
At High Noon

The Contracting Parties—Ceremony—Toilets—Reception and Invited
Guests

The nuptials of Miss Nellie Smith and Mr. Charlemagne Tower Jr. were
celebrated at high noon today, at the house of the parents of the bride, on
Castro Street. Within the elegant mansion of Mr. and Mrs. G. Frank Smith
the curtains were drawn and the gas burned brilliantly at midday. The chandeliers shed their rays upon a happy scene. There was assembled a numerous
company of the relatives and friends of the contracting parties, the bride being
a favorite in Oakland society. The several apartments had been handsomely
decorated and the floors canvassed. Over the archways of the entrance was
trailing ivy and about the chandeliers were twined strings of smilax. Flowers
and tropical plants lent luxuriance to the ornamentation, and a massive marriage bell was suspended in the parlor.

THE CEREMONY

At 12 noon, as the strains of Mendelssohn's wedding march sounded, the
bridal party entered the parlor, the bride leaning upon the arm of her father,
and the groom escorting the bride's mother. The bridesmaids were the Misses
Ada and Gertrude Smith, sisters of the bride. The grooms men were Mr.
Hugh Vail and Mr. L.F.Codogon. There awaited the bride at the altar Miss
Edith Rising, Miss May Keeler, Miss Erimin Tucker, Miss Gertrude Gordon,
Miss Emma Doherty, Miss Dora Vassault, Miss Anna Cope and Miss Mary
Gamble.

The maids of honor held bright ribbons radiating from the marriage bell.
As the bride and groom took their places under the marriage bell, Miss Alice
Dyer sang "Call Me Thine Own," and the music played softly while the con-
tracting parties knelt at the altar.

The beautiful and impressive marriage service of the Episcopal Church was
performed by Rev. Dr. Henry D. Lathrop of the Church of the Advent,
assisted by the Rev. Dr. Benjamin Akerly of St. John's Church. When the
vows had been taken, and sealed with the wedding ring, they were pronounced man and wife, and the strains of the wedding march from "Lohen-

grin" burst forth. The friends then pressed forward to present their congratulations.

The bride, a charming *chatlain*, looked lovely in white faille, Francaise court train; pearl trimming and full veil;coiffure, high; ornaments, diamonds. The costumes of the sisters of the bride, the bride's mother and the ladies in waiting were rich and elegant.

After the guests had paid their compliments to the happy pair they repaired to the dining room, which was daintily decorated, where a sumptuous wedding breakfast was served.

THE CONTRACTING PARTIES

The bride, formerly Miss Nellie Smith, is a daughter of Mr. and Mrs. G. Frank Smith, her father being a leading San Francisco attorney residing in this city. She is a young lady of rare personal charm and amiability of character. The bride was born in San Francisco, but her home has been in Oakland several years past and she graduated from Snell Seminary.

The groom, Mr. Charlemagne Tower Jr., is a resident of Philadelphia. He has been for five years past president of the Duluth and Iron Range railroad and managing director of the Minnesota Iron Company, which position he has lately given up to assume the management of the Finance Company of Pennsylvania, one of the leading banking institutions of Philadelphia, of which Horton Barker is president. Mr. Tower has visited California on several occasions, and it was upon one of these visits that he formed the acquaintance of the young lady whom he has made his wife.

THE GUESTS

Although the invitations were limited to relatives and immediate friends of the contracting parties, there were a large number present. Among those invited were many friends of the family from San Francisco and leading society people of this city. The list of invited guests numbers about 150. In compliance with the desire of the family, the list of guests is not given.

There were many elegant and costly presents received from the friends and families, among them a solid silver service, several sets of silver knives and spoons and sets of rare china, antique vases, paintings, bric-a-brac, and articles of use and ornamentation.

The bride and groom left this afternoon on their wedding tour. Mr. and Mrs. C. Tower, after passing their honeymoon in southern California, will reside permanently in Philadelphia.

Nellie and Charlie's first stop on their wedding trip was the Hotel Del Monte, in Monterey, California, where they received letters from Nellie's mother and sisters as well as telegrams which had arrived after their departure. After a two-week stay in southern California they went by train across the country, arriving in New York on March 1.

On the evening of their arrival, Charlie wrote to his youngest sister, Grace Tower Putnam, to whom he was particularly close:

New York, Thursday evening

1 March, 1888
My dear Grace,

Nellie and I arrived in New York this evening after our long journey, safely and well. We heard yesterday in Chicago, by a letter from Deborah, of the birth of your little son, at which we are delighted and we hasten to send you our love and warmest congratulations. Tell Earl also that we are very happy for him in this event.

We shall stay in New York about a week, at the Buckingham Hotel, and then go to Philadelphia for good. In the mean time we shall go to Philadelphia on Saturday, to see the family and to spend the day with them, returning here by a late train in the evening.

Our wedding was very handsome and impressive. I wish very much you could have seen it, no doubt you would have thought it rather strange to see your big brother going through the ceremony, but I did it all right, as it seems, and everybody appeared entirely contented. Nellie's presents are very beautiful, and there are a great many of them. I hope you will see them in Philadelphia before long. I shall have to tell you about all this when I see you, and Nellie will have much also to talk to you about.

I am very happily married, Grace. This loving and generous-hearted girl fulfills my ideal entirely. I feel that my life must be better and stronger for being passed with her. I am contented more and more every day for having taken the step.

You will judge for yourself when you see her. She is prepared to love you and I am sure you must return her affection.

Much love to you and Earl,
Your affectionate brother, Charlie

11

Rittenhouse Square, 1888–1896

Nellie and Charlie moved into their new home in Philadelphia, at 243 South 18th Street on Rittenhouse Square, in the middle of March 1888, but it would be several months before they were completely settled.

Charlie's parents, Amelia and Charlemagne, lived a few blocks away at 1525 Spruce Street. The two families visited back and forth as much as Charlemagne's failing health would allow. Family groups frequently included Charlie's sister Emma who lived in nearby Pottsville with her husband and two children, and Charlie's unmarried sister Henrietta "Ettie," who lived at home with her parents.

While Neliie settled down to her social rounds and the pleasure of running her own household for the first time, Charlie went each day to his job at the Finance Company of Pennsylvania. In addition to his position in the bank, Charlie had another salaried job—he was a member of the executive committee for the Minnesota Mining and Railroad Syndicate for which he attended periodic meetings in New York and Chicago.

Nellie was sorely missed in Oakland, especially by her father. In the following letter, marked by her on the envelope "Save Always," he showed a remarkable understanding of what Nellie must have experienced meeting the Tower family and being introduced to Philadelphia society:

> San Francisco, March 5th 1888
> My Darling daughter
> 3000 miles away! What a complete separation! How hard to realize that our Nell has flown so far from the parent nest! That henceforth her sympathies and motives must be upon a different plane from the loved ones at home....Father lives in sweet memories of the past, and your unfailing love, brightness and companionship will keep your place warm in his heart...
> By this time you have met your husband's relatives, and the occultism of first impressions have already written chapter 1 in the book of your future lives. I will not ask how you liked them, or they you, for you are too well bred to have allowed any shadows to obscure the smiling good will and seeming

pleasure of a first meeting, but I do inquire as to the degree of appreciation, and relative preferences. Which sister did you like best? Will the old gentleman take my place? Can Mrs. Tower supply the yearnings of your heart for a mother's love? What were your interpretations of Uncle Reuben's character? Is he what we fancied—warm hearted but eccentric, or like Irving, Swift and Byron, the victim of a blighted heart "Pensive sojourners in a world of shadows."?...

If all the people call on you that threaten to, your social duties will be no sinecure—however for a time Californians will be welcome guests...

We have heard from the boys in Guatemala, and their letters overflow with affectionate and appreciative praises of their dear little Nellie. Percy says that Mr. Tower is a very fortunate man to have won the love of so noble a woman and Bert thinks that sister of his is worth more than millions to any man, he seems to be in some doubt whether a stranger can appreciate her real value; and says that she has all the virtues, and not a single fault...

Goodbye, my own darling daughter. Give my kind regards to your husband, and for yourself receive love and kisses from,
Your own dear
Papa

In June of 1888 Nellie and Charlie moved for the summer to a house on the outskirts of the city, on School Lane in Germantown. On weekday mornings the coachman drove Charlie to the train station from which he commuted to center Philadelphia. Nellie was by now in the early months of pregnancy and the cooler country air was a welcome relief from the city in mid summer, and considered much healthier as well.

The senior Towers spent the summer at the Homestead in Waterville, New York, to which they traveled by train, accompanied by their daughter, Ettie. Amelia wrote to her new daughter-in-law from Waterville on July 23, 1888:

My Dear Nellie,
You have for this present time missed seeing us here in our beautiful home. This old home has stood on the same grounds, as a glorious home for the Tower children and grandchildren, for many long, long years, and is just the same in grandness and welcome as when it was first put under roof...Many of the old red and white beech and cherry birch trees—brought here by the Indians, and planted, call my children under their clean cool shade, with the same voice of kind welcome which has ever sounded from their handsome dark green leaves, to "come and sit in the shade and enjoy yourselves."

Now, my dear girl, this little call has been made to you and Charlie. I have heard this leaf language and understood the call, every morning; and so you both come, when you can do so.

I wish I could find something pretty to send you. I have looked around in our gay garden, and shall send you this *Cana indica*. It is very beautiful and showy...

My dear Nellie, this is to you from your affectionate Mother and true friend,

Amelia M. Tower

Nellie wrote to her parents in California on September 2, 1888, her thirtieth birthday, with the happy news of her pregnancy. She urged her mother to make the trip East to be with her at the baby's arrival.

Her mother received the letter on September 10; she answered the same day:

The letter from your sweet self, written on your birthday, came this morning, the contents of which nearly took away my breath...I cried and laughed alternately.

God grant you strength and health, to be carried through this happy period, and a child be given you, to rise up and call you blessed and make your home a perfect one. I can scarcely write I am so happy, and so over come by the good tidings.

When Amelia Tower received Nellie's happy news in Waterville, she, too, replied immediately:

September 23, 1888

My Dear Nellie,

I have your letter of the 19th...I am glad to receive from you, as I have been many times before...this kind of an annunciation letter from my dear daughters. Allow me, my dear girl, to add you as one more strong gold link to this lovely chain of dutiful and affectionate children. This beautiful chain has controlled and shaped my life, and is the altar on which I find much strength and happiness.

I shall go with you in Spirit through the coming months, and shall help to make your journey a quiet "pleasure trip" as far as can be in my power.

I have made so many little Babe "Out Fits" and am well acquainted in this pleasure work. I will now say to you, Nellie, if you will give me the happy commission, or order, I will fill it in full.

Affectionately your Mother,

Amelia M. Tower

Nellie and Charlie's baby would be the sixth grand child for Amelia and Charlemagne, but the first one to bear the Tower name.

The young couple did visit Waterville in October of 1888. On the way home to Philadelphia, Charlie researched the most comfortable route for his father and mother for their return a few weeks later. His father's health was precarious; he would need to rest constantly on the trip home.

On his return to Philadelphia, Charlie contacted the Pullman Company and leased a private two-bedroom railroad car that would be attached to a train at Waterville and would take them through to Philadelphia.

On February 8, 1889, Nellie and Charlie's first wedding anniversary, Nellie's mother wrote a letter to accompany a quilt that she had made for the baby:

My Dear Darling Nell,

Many returns of the anniversary day which though it took you from us, brought so much happiness into your life. God grant it may grow fuller, and richer, every day you live and that both husband and children, may "rise up and call you blessed."

The little eider down quilt is all mother's handiwork and is intended to throw over the "little fellow" when he is reposing. Every stitch is worked in love, and you must accept it not with a critic's eye, but because it brings with it the earnest wish for the darling's happiness and expresses the joy of all of us in possessing a share in the treasure.

Take good care of yourself, dear Neno, and with best love to yourself, and Charlemagne on this Anniversary occasion, believe me always and forever,

Your devoted
Mother

12

Family Matters

By the middle of March 1889, the house on Rittenhouse Square was bustling with preparations for the new baby. Nellie's mother had arrived from California. Nellie had hired Miss Roberts, an experienced baby nurse with excellent references. Miss Roberts's domain, the nursery, was a confection of lace and ribbons, the bassinet fit for royalty. Drawers overflowed with little hand-made outfits with tiny buttons and fine stitching made by both grandmothers, aunts and close friends.

On Wednesday, March 20, a clear, sunny day, Nellie, Charlemagne, and Nellie's mother were enjoying a carriage ride in the park when Nellie had the first indication that the baby was on its way. Charlemagne directed the coachman to drive home at a swift, but safe, speed. As soon as they reached home, he called the family physician, Dr. Bennett.

At 6:30 the next morning a baby boy arrived, weighing seven pounds. His name, which had been determined many months before, would be Charlemagne Tower III. His proud parents could not take their eyes off him. The two grandmothers pronounced him the most perfect of babies.

The rest of the Tower family were fairly giddy with relief that the baby had not been a girl, and that now the Tower name would be carried on. Henrietta Tower Page, Charlie's seventy-five year-old aunt, expressed the family's feelings on the matter:

> Waterville, March 23, 1889
> My Dear Charlie,
>   We were sincerely glad to receive your letter Thursday evening, and rejoice with you, and Nellie, in the birth of a son, Charlemagne Tower 3rd. As I read your letter a <u>momentary</u> feeling of anxiety came over me, lest it should be a daughter. It was my strong wish for a son to bear the family name. Forgive me for my pride, dear Charlie, while I hope <u>he</u> will always be called by his full name. I love the little one, already, and hope to see the little fellow many times myself.

It would have gratified you, could you have seen the pleasure your Uncle Reuben evinced at the birth of your child...

With much love to both you, and Nellie, I am,

Your Affectionate

Aunt Henrietta

The christening of Charlemagne Tower III took place on April 18, his Grandfather Charlemagne Tower's 80th birthday. The baby's father, Charlie, whose birthday was the day before, had just turned 41. [1]

Nellie's sister, Floie, and her husband, LeRoy, came from California for the event, and Debbie, Charlie's sister, and her husband, Dick Lee, came from Duluth to join all of the Philadelphia family in the celebration. Nellie wrote to her sister, Adabelle, in California, to share her happiness:

243 So. 18—Rittenhouse Square
Monday, April 1, 4.30 P.M.

My Dearest Oddie,

This is the first time I have taken pen in hand to write since the eventful night which preceded the birth of our boy; the letter I sent Gertie that night represents the Omega of my girlhood—this to you darling Oddie the Alpha of my motherhood.

Oh! How many, many times Mama and I have talked of our precious dear ones and I think our desire to have you all see and love our "little fellow" intensifies every hour...I still realize so little that he is <u>mine,</u> ours, forever! A little immortal soul—a new joy—a son! It is too much happiness.

Darling Toodles [Nellie's mother] has been such a comfort and delight to me during these long convalescing hours when I have been made to lie down and rest all day. Now I have my liberty again though in a measured degree, and I can wander from room to room on this floor...

Even the Doctor may be partial but he says <u>our</u> baby is "unusually bright and wide-awake"...When he makes a little sound we all exclaim with delight—when he looks at us out of his big blue eyes, we watch for a change of expression with perfect fascination and as for his little morning bath that is the wonder of the day...

A new expression of a new-found joy has come into Charlemagne's face whenever he approaches our boy...

Your devoted sister, Nellie

---

1.   Details of family life at the birth of Charlemagne III come from a baby book with entries written by both parents. Written in the first person, the little book was meant to sound as if the baby himself had dictated it.

On Sunday mornings as the weather grew warmer, Charlie, Nellie and Miss Roberts would walk over to see Charlie's parents at 1525 Spruce Street. The baby was passed around from one adoring relative to another, starting with his grandfather, then his grandmother, then his aunts Emmie and Ettie. On one visit, when Charlemagne senior was especially weak, Charlie placed the baby next to him on the bed and the infant went to sleep firmly holding his grandfather's finger.

On May 30th the senior Towers took the train to Waterville for the summer, accompanied by Ettie. Charlemagne's parting words to Nellie were, "take good care of that dear boy."

On June 6, Charlie and Nellie again moved their household to School House Lane for the summer. Nellie, writing in the baby book, described the Germantown house as the "dear old-fashioned house painted in white stucco with a circular porch and white pillars and great spreading lawns and mammoth old trees with a wide vine-covered veranda at the back...", under which the baby could nap in his carriage.

School Lane, Germantown, Pennlylvania, 1890.
Nellie and Charlemagne leased this house
for the summer, then moved back to Rittenhouse Square in
November. The baby on Nellie's lap is Dominie.

On July 19th Charlie was suddenly called to Waterville; his father was very ill and had slipped into a coma. Charlie sent Nellie telegrams every day. As his father's end drew near, he wrote Nellie:

> Waterville, 24 July, 1889, Wednesday evening.
> My dearest Nellie,
>   I hope you are getting along well all this time that I am obliged to be away, and I know you will be brave and patient. This is a trial to us all. My dear Father is breathing out his life. He lies unconscious, free from pain, almost as if he were in a natural sleep. His face is beautiful, filled with that noble kindness and tenderness that we all remember so well in days gone by. He does not look feeble or old—you would not imagine him to be eighty years of age. He is surrounded by his family, who are doing all that affectionate solicitude can suggest. But he is dying. I never wrote so sad a word before—no doubt you are prepared for this, by the news I have sent you from day to day in my telegrams. And it is true, the end has come.
>   How wonderful that after all his long life and his varied experience in the world, he should come back to the old homestead to die; where his Father was buried more than fifty years ago and his mother lived, and died. And he will be laid in the little graveyard where his Grandparents are also—It seems a fitting end, and the peaceful air of everything about the place today with the sun shining brightly upon it and coming in at the windows he loved so to look out of and falling now upon his deathbed, seems like a benediction upon this beautiful and well spent life.
>   My heart is full—you know how we loved him. You can estimate his loss. We shall tell our little boy of him, in the years to come, we shall teach him by his example. During his last conscious moments he asked for you and little Charlemagne, and almost with his last strength he raised his hand and smiling, pointed to the little lock of the baby's hair that hangs framed opposite his bed...
>   Good night, my Darlings—Love to you both,
>   From your affectionate, C.

Charlemagne Tower died in Waterville late in the evening on Wednesday, July 24, 1889, at the age of eighty. His funeral was held on Saturday, July 27, at the Homestead. He was buried in the Tower family plot in the Waterville Cemetery across a deep ravine from the Homestead. In winter, Charlemagne's monument could be seen from the east windows of the house.

At the time of Charlemagne's death, five of his seven siblings were still living: his brothers Julius, James, Francis M. and Reuben, and his only sister, Henrietta Tower Page.

Charlemagne Tower's obituaries told of a life lived to the fullest. Two of his riskiest ventures were taken on when he was considered by many to be too old for the challenge at hand. The first was leaving his law practice in Pottsville, Pennsylvania, to recruit and lead a militia company in the first year of the Civil War when he was fifty-two years old.

The second occurred when, in his late sixties, he mortgaged everything he owned to start a company to mine iron ore in the Vermilion Range in Minnesota. The success of this venture made him a millionaire when he was well into his seventies.[2]

Charlemagne's widow, Amelia, his son Charlemagne junior [at his father's death, Charlie began referring to himself as Charlemagne—for the purposes of this narrative, Charlie will be referred to as Charlemagne from this point on], and his four daughters, Deborah, Emma, Henrietta and Grace, and their heirs, would benefit from a trust which would continue for the next one hundred years.

After ten days in Waterville, young Charlemagne returned to Philadelphia and the happy routines of fatherhood. In the late afternoon when he returned from the railroad station by horse drawn carriage, he would pick up his little son, now called Dominie, and hold him while he patted the horses.

On November 4, the young Towers moved their household from School Lane back to Rittenhouse Square. Later in the month, Nellie's dear friend Mrs. Colton came from California for a week's visit.

For Nellie, this visit must have been a special pleasure. Mrs. Colton had always been kind and generous to Nellie and her sisters. Now Nellie could shower her friend with lavish hospitality.

In December, Nellie realized that she was pregnant again; the baby was due in late June. If she wanted to visit her family in California she would have to make the trip soon. She and Charlemagne decided that she should spend the winter in California; Charlemagne would join her there at the beginning of March.

Nellie left Philadelphia on Saturday, December 28, with little Dominie and the nurse, Ellen, for what turned out to be a hazardous trip. The train was delayed by a major storm in the Rocky Mountains. Then as they neared Oakland on Thursday, Jan 3, the train slowed to a crawl as it pushed through heavy snow drifts on the outskirts of the city.

---

2.   In *Iron Millionaire: The Life of Charlemagne Tower,* author Hal Bridges chronicled Charlemagne Tower Senior's successful venture in the mining of iron ore.

Nellie did not return to the house on Castro street which had been sold shortly after her wedding. Her parents now lived in the coastal town of Bolinas just north of San Francisco. On week days her father stayed at the Hotel Pleasanton in San Francisco.

At the end of February, Charlemagne wrote Nellie that he would be unable to join her in California after all. She cut short her trip, spent ten days at the Palace Hotel in San Francisco seeing old friends, and departed for the four-day and five-night trip to Chicago where Charlemagne would meet her. Her train arrived twenty-four hours late due to engine failure crossing the Rockies. It was the middle of March before Nellie, Dominie and nurse Ellen arrived home in Philadelphia once again. Nellie was by now in her sixth month of pregnancy.

During her California visit, Nellie could not help but notice her family's reduced circumstances. Her father had put several years of effort and a substantial amount of money in a single case, Colton v. The Southern Pacific Railroad. He represented the family's friend, Mrs. Colton, in the suit on a contingent fee basis, shouldering all of the financial outlay himself. He and five associates won the case in the Superior Court in Santa Rosa, but the defendants took the case to the Supreme Court.

It was in late May that Nellie heard that the California Supreme Court had overturned the decision and her father had lost the case. It was a devastating reversal. She feared that her father would be left destitute. She wrote to her father immediately; on June 11, 1890, he answered her letter:

> San Francisco
> My darling Nellie,
>   You are desirous of knowing what my plans and prospects are, and we have endeavored to keep to ourselves details that might worry you, without in any possible manner benefiting ourselves by their disclosure. The end of the Colton case gave us a staggering blow that it will take a year or two to recover from, but I have the energy, and just the family to lift a fellow to his legs again—so no one despairs…
>   Our judicial system has grown so vilely corrupt, that leading lawyers are leaving the profession, and I am so thoroughly disgusted with law and its unfair administration that I have determined if possible to find some more creditable manner of supporting my family.
>   With this view I interested a large capitalist here (S.J.Drexler) who is my intimate friend, in the purchase of one or more coffee fincas [plantations] in Guatemala, which I was to take charge of, and manage on shares, but the present high price of coffee has so boomed this property, that it is almost impossible to purchase a plantation at any figure, and quite impossible to get one at a reasonable price.

Within the last 18 months fincas have changed hands at double, and even treble, previous prices, which inflation is owing to the immense demand for coffee land there, by English and German capitalists—Americans are also large purchasers...Percy and Bert have been for the last three months looking up purchasable fincas, but proprietors have uniformly refused to sell, so we have for the present given up all prospects of finding a suitable purchase.

Having temporarily failed in the Guatemala scheme, I am now trying to find some other avenue of employment, though of course not a clerkship. I am a good accountant and bookkeeper—a thorough business man, industrious, and honest, all of which ought to bring me the desired occupation—in the meantime I practice as little law as possible, but still enough to keep the wolf from our door.

Now little pet, you have the whole story, but don't worry over <u>our affairs</u>. We will get along, and whether rich or poor, we will always be the same proud, exclusive and highly respectable family—asking no favors and accepting assistance from <u>nobody.</u>

You know how strong my belief is in fatalism—and my perfect confidence that "what is to be will be" for "There is a providence that shapes our course..."

On July 1, 1890, Nellie gave birth to another seven-pound boy, this time in the School House Lane house. Again, she was attended by Dr. Bennett and the baby went into the care of Miss Roberts.

Nellie and Charlemagne named the baby Geoffrey. Little Dominie, now a toddler of 16 months, was walking confidently and beginning to say a few words. Two little boys now shared the spotlight.

The Tower family spent the month of August at Elberon on the New Jersey Shore. Now it was Geoffrey's baby book in which family life was recorded: "We all had a happy month at Elberon having a cottage all to ourselves, our own horses, butler and the two nurses, Ellen and Miss Roberts."

Geoffrey was christened on September 24, 1890. Emma and Tom Snyder were his godparents; they and six guests attended the ceremony. Charlemagne resigned his position as Vice President of the Finance Company of Pennsylvania, because in April 1891 he and Nellie took the two little boys and their nurses to Europe for six months. They spent four months on the Continent, then settled down in the Cotswolds to explore England for two months. Nellie, who counted travel as one of the things she had always wanted most, was blissfully happy in the double joy of seeing new places and having her little family with her.

A year later, early in the summer of 1892, Charlemagne, Nellie and nurses Bessie and Agnes took the boys to California to visit Nellie's family. This was the last time Nellie saw her mother, who died shortly after Nellie's trip. In October,

Nellie was confined with another birth, that of a third son, Roderick, born on October 21, 1892.

Life in Philadelphia was pleasant indeed. The Tower household on Rittenhouse Square now had three little boys in residence and at least as many nurses, in addition to the kitchen help, maids, footmen, butler, groom and coachman.

Charlemagne had many interests: he was a director of the American Institute of Mining Engineers and served on the boards of two railroads. He was a trustee of the University of Pennsylvania and president of its department of Archaeology and Paleontology, and a member of both the Academy of Natural Sciences and the Historical Society of Pennsylvania. He also served as one of three trustees for his father's estate.

Nellie had mastered the once daunting Philadelphia social conventions and was by now a relaxed and gracious hostess. She and Charlemagne entertained whenever trips to California and her frequent confinements permitted. In May 1893, the Towers invited friends to a tea dance to be held at the Germantown Cricket Club on Thursday, May 25th.

For five years Charlemagne had been at work on a book about the Marquis de Lafayette and the important role the young Frenchman played in the American Revolution. The subject appealed to him on several levels—he was devoted to the study of American history and he was interested in all things French. He read and spoke French fluently, which helped considerably with his research.

At that time Charlemagne's book was the first biography of Lafayette that focused on his activities in the American Revolution. Charlemagne went to great lengths to borrow and to acquire unpublished letters that he used to chronicle Lafayette's day-to-day movements.

Early in 1894 Lippincott published Charlemagne's work as a two-volume history, *The Marquis de Lafayette in the American Revolution.* The book received good reviews and Charlemagne was soon in demand as a guest lecturer on American history at historical societies, universities and at the Naval War College in Newport, Rhode Island.

On April 9, 1894 Nellie's father, G. Frank Smith, died in San Francisco. His obituary in the *San Francisco Chronicle* cited many of his better-known cases, some of them notable successes, including one involving the heirs of Mark Hopkins. The newspapers described Frank Smith as a man who had made and lost many fortunes and who was admired for his equanimity in the face of adversity.

Nellie was visiting her father when he died. As she was expecting her fourth child in June, she spent several winter months in California with the little boys and their nurses. When her father became ill she postponed her departure and Charlemagne joined her in Santa Barbara for the birth of their fourth child.

The baby was a girl, whom they named Helen, born on June 27th. The boys were now five, four and two.

Losses of members of the older generation continued through the next several years. In April, 1896, Charlemagne's mother, Amelia Malvina Tower, died in Philadelphia at the age of seventy-seven. As had happened at the deaths of Charlemagne senior in 1889, Susan Smith in 1892, and Frank Smith in 1894, there was a Tower baby born to Nellie and Charlemagne the same year.

On October 30, 1896, a second daughter, Gertrude, arrived, joining four older siblings—Dominie, 7, Geoffrey, 6, Roderick, just 4, and Helen, 2.

Charlemagne had for some time been considering a career in diplomacy. With business successes in Duluth and in Philadelphia behind him, an ample income, and, since the publication of his work on Lafayette, a new reputation as a historian, Charlemagne was well qualified for a diplomatic appointment at a high level.

He was also a generous supporter of the Republican Party in general, and in particular to the campaign of William McKinley. When McKinley won the presidential election in 1897, Charlemagne let it be known to the Pennsylvania senators Boise Penrose and Matthew S. Quay that he would be interested in a diplomatic appointment.

13

Vienna 1897–1899

Nellie Tower, Vienna, 1897.

Passport photos of Tower children for move to Vienna in 1897

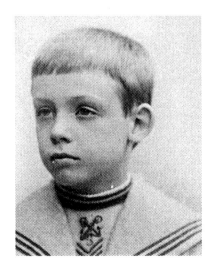

Dominie, 8

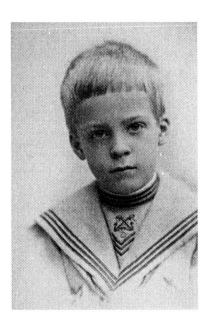

Geoffrey, 7

Roderick, 5

Helen, 3

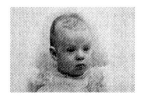

Gertrude, 7 months

Nellie and Charlemagne Tower on the terrace of
their Vienna home, the Palais Springer, 1897.

Drawing room, Palais Springer, Vienna
1897.

Vienna, 1898—from left, Roderick, Helen, Dominie and Geoffrey holding
the reins.

President McKinley's advisors found in Charlemagne Tower an ideal candidate for a diplomatic assignment. By the age of forty-eight he had distinguished himself in both business and literature. He had an excellent education at Exeter and Harvard enhanced by four years of study and travel abroad. He spoke fluent French, the language of diplomacy, as well as German and Spanish. As an attorney, he took a particular interest in international law.

As a young man, Charlemagne had even held a minor diplomatic post— during his first year of travel after college, in the winter of 1872-73, he served as the attaché to the American Legation under General Daniel E. Sickles, United States Minister to Spain.

In the following four-year period, he studied in Paris, at Tours, and at Frankfurt on Main, lived in Egypt for a year and traveled throughout the Middle East. The prolonged period of travel and study gave him a significant understanding of regional politics.

Another important factor in Charlemagne's favor was his independent income. If nominated, he could afford to augment the meager diplomatic salary from his own pocket. A substantial private income was essential in a major diplomatic post if the ambassador were to do more than simply maintain the embassy staff and live frugally.

Certainly one of Charlemagne's greatest assets as a prospective diplomat was Nellie. At thirty-eight, Nellie was still slender and had a flair for dressing which was much admired. She had great poise and was tactful and considerate of others and she was blessed with both good health and abundant energy that enabled her to manage her flock of small children, run her household and still maintain her place in society.

When senators Penrose and Quay started pressing the President's advisors for a diplomatic appointment for Charlemagne Tower, they hoped for the position of Ambassador to Berlin. But it was thought that Charlemagne was not well known enough in diplomatic circles to merit a major post right away.

President McKinley announced Charlemagne's appointment as Minister to Austria-Hungary in January 1897, and his nomination was subsequently approved by the Senate in early April. The major city newspapers in New York and Philadelphia viewed the nomination favorably, but the pundits at some smaller newspapers had a good time poking fun at the unknown candidate with the long name.

The Times-Union of Jacksonville, Florida wrote on April 7, 1887: "Shakespeare would not have sneeringly asked, 'What's in a name?' had he known that Charlemagne Tower was going to get such an important foreign appointment."

The Leader, Cleveland, Ohio, noted in its March 31, 1887 edition: "Charle-magne Tower, of Pennsylvania, to be Envoy Extraordinary and Minister Plenipo-tentiary! How is that for a collection of big names?"

Congratulations poured in from well-wishers among Charlemagne's acquain-tances. The Union League Club of Philadelphia gave a dinner for him, and on April 29, The Historical Society of Pennsylvania hosted a large farewell dinner at which he was the guest speaker.

The Department of State sent a letter of credit dated April 13, 1897 to Brown, Shipley & Co., London, for a yearly salary of $12,000 plus "Contingent Expenses of the Legation not to exceed $2,300." Charlemagne's yearly income from his father's estate was $48,000 a year. Over time, the diplomatic life would seriously erode his personal wealth.

Nellie directed the closing of the Philadelphia house and chose the furnishings they would ship to Vienna. It would be hard leaving the big comfortable house on Rittenhouse Square that held years of happy memories. Nellie could recite from memory passages from Charlemagne's letters written during their engage-ment describing the house to her. He had labored over the color schemes for the various rooms, trying to find the perfect combination. She well remembered the excitement of shopping in New York for furniture for their new home, and lamps, and pictures and carpets. Never had she spent so much money in such a short time in her life.

Most of all, the house was the home of her little family, where the nursery was never empty and where the older children had taken their first steps. Baby Ger-trude would learn to walk somewhere in Vienna.

The Tower family had planned to sail to Europe on Wednesday, May 5, 1897, on the American steamer *St. Paul*, but two days before they were due to leave, the children came down with whooping cough. The passage had to be can-celed. Charlemagne was finally able to find space on the English White Star steamer, *The Majestic*, by booking a group of cabins which could be quarantined.

As the *Majestic* got under way, Charlemagne received a telegram from Captain Harlow of the Flagship *New York*: "When you pass the Flagship *New York* our band will play the *Austrian National Aire* and *Auld Lang Syne* as an act of courtesy by direction of the Commander in Chief."

The children settled into their shipboard infirmary, supervised by their nurses and their parents. Dominie, the oldest, had just turned eight; Geoffrey would be seven in July; Roderick was five and a half; Helen would be three in June and baby Gertrude was seven months old.

An exhausted group of adults and children arrived in Vienna in the middle of May; they stayed at the Hotel Bristol while they looked for a suitable house.

It was the most beautiful time of year for Nellie's first visit to Vienna. The many parks and Danube canals made driving around the city a pleasure. Along the Ringstrasse, a broad tree-lined boulevard that circled the old city, Emperor Franz Joseph had created new public buildings in various styles of classic architecture. Vienna's two most spectacular palaces, the Belvedere Palace and the fourteen-hundred-room Schonbrunn Palace had formal gardens that rivaled Versailles.

Emperor Franz Joseph, then in the fiftieth year of his reign[1], ruled an empire that extended from the Swiss border to the Ukraine. The short form of his title, used by the State Department in its letter of introduction for Charlemagne, was *His Majesty Francis Joseph, Emperor of Austria, King of Bohemia and Apostolic King of Hungary.* Charlemagne's official title was *Envoy Extraordinary and Minister Plenipotentiary of the United States of America.*

On June 18, 1897, Charlemagne presented his credentials to the Emperor in a formal ceremony at the Hofburg Palace. Charlemagne described the Emperor to Nellie as "extremely dignified with a kind, open face and in excellent health."

Nellie saved the kid gloves Charlemagne wore for the ceremony with a note attached describing his interview with the Emperor. It was considered unusual, she wrote, "in this exclusive court…that the emperor expressed great interest in all the subjects relating to America and smiled with pleasure when in reply to his question he found Charlemagne had brought his five small children to Vienna with him."

Vienna was an agreeable assignment for a first-time diplomat. Relations were good between Austria-Hungary and the United States. Carl Dolmetsch, writing in *"Our Famous Guest" Mark Twain in Vienna,* noted that the Viennese, like other central Europeans, had an "immense curiosity…about America and Americans in the last century…Americans were still exotic creatures, and an educated American of distinction…was the most exotic of all…"[2]

The Towers soon found a house to lease, actually a small palace, at IV Alleegasse 27. Known as Palais Springer, it was described by a Philadelphia newspaper as "the splendid palace of a grand duke in one of the most aristocratic quarters of Vienna. The dining room ceiling is supported by massive red marble pillars. Pic-

---

1.   Emperor Franz Joseph assumed the throne in 1848 at the age of eighteen; he succeeded his feeble minded uncle, Ferdinand I.

2.   Dolmetsch, *Our Famous Guest*, 142.

tures by David Teniers and other famous artists line the walls. The drawing room is furnished in Louis XIV style. There is a delightful little Japanese salon adjoining."[3]

In September of 1897, the American colony found itself making front page news: Samuel Clemens, known throughout Europe as Mark Twain, had come to Vienna for an indefinite stay, with his wife Livy and their two daughters, Clara and Jean. It was the end of a sad year of mourning for the Clemens family, who had lost their daughter, Susy, to spinal meningitis in August of 1896.

Clemens had brought his family to Vienna so that his daughter Clara, a talented pianist, could study with the famous teacher Theodor Letchetisky. The famous author immediately took an interest in every aspect of the life of the city, especially the sessions of the Austrian parliament, the Reichsrat, which he observed from the visitors' gallery.

The Viennese newspapers, of which there were more than one hundred, adored Mark Twain and quoted him on every occasion. The famous Americans and their daughters held court to countless visitors in their spacious suite at the Hotel Metropole and were soon regular visitors at the American Embassy. They were guests of honor at Thanksgiving Dinner on Thursday, November 25, 1897 and attended a large dinner at the embassy residence in February 1898, for the diplomatic community.

The following year, *The Philadelphia Times,* Nov. 26, 1898 described the Thanksgiving dinner at the Towers:

> From Vienna comes the news of a Thanksgiving dinner, given by Minister and Mrs. Charlemagne Tower, of this city, in their palace, for two hundred guests. Mrs. Tower wore a gown of black sprigged net, relieved by masses of palette embroidery, her neck and arms showing through the transparency of the sleeves and high bodice. In her hair she wore black jet ornaments and carried a large bouquet of violets...Mrs. Clemens (Mrs. Mark Twain) wore brocade and gros grain, with appliquéd cloth; Miss Clara Clemens wore black silk and a lavender spencer; Miss Jean Clemens's gown was of dove-gray cashmere...Best known among the guests was Mark Twain, "the lion of the evening..."

The Tower household ran smoothly under Nellie's careful eye. She had arranged for a young English woman, Hester Candler, to join the family in Vienna as governess, as well as a young Englishman named George Webb who would assume various household duties and help care for the little boys.

---

3.   *The American,* Dec. 14, 1898.

Hester and George soon became indispensable. When the Towers traveled without the children, which they did frequently, Hester and George filled in as surrogate parents. Then Hester had complete charge of the household—from footmen and chambermaids to nursemaids and kitchen help while George managed the grooms and stable help and would supervise the little boys when they played outdoors. When the Towers were away from home, Hester wrote Nellie every day, giving a complete report on each child.

This letter, missing its envelope, was probably sent to the Towers on a visit to Paris:

IV AlleeGasse 27

Vienna
February 18th [1898]
My dear Madam
    The children are now in bed and I hasten to write you how the day has passed…after our dinner at midday we started off on our drive. It commenced to snow quite heavily…at the bridge George and the boys and Helen got out and walked over the bridge and some distance along the road, but as the wind was so very strong, baby and I remained in the carriage…She screamed with joy, but it was not very long before the little head sunk down on my shoulder and she slept for quite a long time…Helen and the boys behaved wonderfully well, they were all very merry, made plenty of noise and enjoyed themselves very much. Geoffrey was delighted because he saw a donkey…
Yours very faithfully,
Hester Candler

In the spring of 1898, Charlemagne's unmarried sister, Henrietta, known as Ettie, announced that she would marry George W. Wurts, a retired diplomat who had served in St. Petersburg, Madrid and Rome. Ettie, age fort-one and an heiress in her own right, had taken care of her parents in their old age. The wedding took place on April 12 in Philadelphia at the house on Spruce Street which Ettie had inherited from her parents. The Wurtses went to live in Rome and soon became members of the international set.

Charlemagne was conscientious and painstaking in his official duties. His diplomatic skill became evident in his delicate handling of the American involvement with Cuba in the Spanish American War in 1898. Author Dolmetsch wrote, "American involvement with Cuba had created a tense international crisis by February 1898…Austria-Hungary was even more sympathetic than most of Europe to the Spanish cause, and Tower was able to neutralize some of the anti-American sentiment…by getting Secretary of State John Hay to lobby a bill through Congress exempting Austrians who had become naturalized Americans from military service."[4]

Samuel Clemens considered Charlemagne Tower the ideal diplomat. In a piece written in 1899 by him under his pen name, unpublished at the time and subsequently entitled "American Representation in Austria," Twain stated that Charlemagne Tower possessed all the qualities necessary for the perfect representative of the United States.[5]

The State Department usually reviewed tours of duty every two years. It is probable that Charlemagne's supporters in Philadelphia and Washington were pressing for a post for him as ambassador in one of the big three consulates: Paris, London or Berlin. Charlemagne's first choice was Paris.

That Charlemagne could have been considered for a post as ambassador in a major European capital at this early stage in his diplomatic career points out the extent to which American procedures for diplomatic advancement differed from that of other countries.

The lofty position of ambassador after only a few years in the diplomatic service was possible for Americans. Ambassadorships were rewards for service in other fields—excellence in the arts, education, business or simply as paybacks for campaign contributions. By contrast, career diplomats from other countries spent years in the diplomatic service before they could hope to become ambassador. This often put American diplomats in an awkward position.

Herbert J. Hagerman, in his fine memoir, *Letters of a Young Diplomat*, commented on how the American system affected its diplomats at that time: "American diplomats are everywhere treated with hauteur by their colleagues. They see a man placed in a position which they can only reach after a life spent in the service [and they know he got there] by a mere pronouncement of the President..."[6]

On January 8, 1899, Charlemagne received a telegram from John Hay, Secretary of State: "The President desires to promote you to the Russian Embassy. Will this be agreeable?" Charlemagne wired back from Vienna on January 9: "I thank the President respectfully and I shall be happy to accept his offer of the Russian Embassy."

Charlemagne's old friend, Alvey A. Adee, Second Assistant Secretary of State, writing on January 9, 1899 described the Russian post as "much more important

---

4.   Dolmetsch, 155.
5.   Ibid., Appendix B.
6.   Hagerman, *Letters of a Young Diplomat*, 64.

[than Vienna] and involves such delicate and far reaching questions of policy to be discussed, that it is at least a one hundred per cent promotion."

The official notification to Emperor Franz Joseph came from President McKinley in a letter dated January 19, 1899; Charlemagne took his official leave from the Emperor on February 9, l899. Nellie wrote a note that she kept in her scrapbook, "The Emperor expressed satisfaction at the way in which he had held his position while here and was cordial to Charlemagne."

On February 28, 1899, the American community gave a farewell dinner for the Towers at the Hotel Bristol. Samuel Clemens delivered the farewell address.

Clemens noted that Mr. Tower was "qualified by a knowledge of the languages required by the business and social relationships of his office; by a broad knowledge of affairs; by knowledge of men and the world [and a] a tongue gifted, at need, of that supreme diplomatic eloquence—silence, when silence is the best speech!"

He praised Ambassador Tower for possessing "the [ability to] perceive that his own country and political system did not monopolize all the virtues, but that other countries and systems have not been forgotten of God in these regards…"[7]

Charlemagne made the following reply:

> Ladies and Gentlemen.—There is really but one thing that I can say to you in return for all this kindness,—Mrs. Tower and I thank you. The proof of good will that you have given us this evening has touched our hearts. It is a souvenir that we shall carry with us from Vienna and cherish in the time to come.
>
> The diplomatic career is, from the nature of the case, full of uncertainties; and like all our lives, exposed to the changes which any day may bring forth, but which no man can foretell. But how true it is that they who go across the seas change, indeed, the skies under which they live, but not the essential qualities of heart and mind. For, kindred spirits meet and form attachments, wherever they may be, the world over. The assurance of this will be to us one of most grateful memories of Vienna. Mrs. Tower and I came here as strangers; you gave us your friendship; and our stay has been made happier and enriched by it.
>
> The hurrying events of the last two years have followed each other in very rapid succession, and I have no doubt that many of you have shared the anxiety that I have felt, at times, myself. But I am glad to tell you now that all is well. And I am sure I shall not betray state secrets if I say to you that the relations between the Government of His Majesty the Emperor and the United States are those of entire cordiality, indeed, that have never been better since the establishment of the commonwealth. So that my successor, whom you will

---

7.   From a copy of Samuel Clemens's address in the author's collection.

see in a few weeks, and who is, I am told, an able and cultivated man will have a new book and a clean page to begin with. It would be difficult for a new-comer to find ready for him a fairer field in which to lay the foundation of a successful mission.

What a beautiful and interesting land this Austria-Hungary is! We have seen it all too little, perhaps, because time would not permit. Yet we have been to Budapest, and Prague, and seen the Danube from Linz; we know the Salz-kammergut, and…Tschl and Salzburg; the lovely region of Reicheman and Kaiserbrunn, and we have gone up over the Summering into Steiermark and down to Graz. Surely there is no more attractive country upon the continent of Europe; a land capable of almost unlimited development, and worthy of a great and brilliant future, which I most earnestly hope it may attain!

And now I look upon your faces gathered about this table I cannot help thinking of the pity of it that this chapter has come to an end. I console myself with the thought, however, that, than not to have had it at all, I would far rather have enjoyed it, even at the cost of the sacrifice which it entails…

14

St. Petersburg 1899–1900

When Charlemagne arrived in St. Petersburg in the winter of 1899, the Neva River and its many canals were frozen solid. A bone-chilling wind blew from the Gulf of Finland, covering and bridges with snow, but the city, sometimes called the Venice of the North, was beautiful at any time of year, even in the grip of winter. Founded in 1703 by Peter the Great who wished to create a capital that would resemble a European city, St. Petersburg's architecture was primarily Baroque and Neoclassical. A network of handsome stone bridges spanned the canals and connected the tree-lined streets.

The new ambassador's first call was at the American Embassy offices, called the Chancellerie, recently vacated by his predecessor, Ambassador Ethan A. Hitchcock who had been recalled by President McKinley to assume the cabinet post of Secretary of the Interior. The First Secretary of the Embassy, Herbert H. D. Peirce, and the Second Secretary, Herbert J. Hagerman would remain on the embassy staff.

The spacious offices of the Chancellerie [1] on the Quai de La Cour took up the entire third floor of a palace belonging to Grand Duke Vladimir, a few blocks from the Winter Palace. Broad windows gave a view across the frozen River Neva to the Citadel of St. Peter and St. Paul.

Charlemagne's first challenge was to find a house for his family. Secretary Peirce had begun working on the housing question as soon as Charlemagne's appointment was announced. In the following letter, part of a continuing correspondence on the subject of housing and other domestic issues, Peirce wrote to Charlemagne on February 27, 1899, concerning a house for rent. This letter concerns a house for rent owned by a family named von Devries. Without the owners' knowledge, their agent, Pomerantzoff, had inflated the yearly rent.

---

1.   The former palace, now called the House of Sciences, houses a scientific conference
      center and apartments.

My dear Mr. Tower,

...I received yesterday an intimation from Mrs. von Devries that the house could be got at a price below what has been asked...that they would be glad to rent the house which costs them 10,000 rubles[2] a year and they were shocked at the price which Mr. Pomrantzoff had put on it. They asked to be informed how much you felt willing to pay...

I have engaged a pair of horses and coupe...The horses are better than the coupe which while new is of Russian make and not entirely ideal. It is so late in the season that there is little choice left...I think you will perhaps find when you get here that it would be at least as economical and more satisfactory to buy your carriages abroad.

You would be able to sell them to good advantage when you are through with them and you could hire the horses alone at a price which would show a large saving even when taking interest and wear and tear into account.

I have engaged the whole outfit including coupe, sledge, coachman and horses at 275 rubles per month with the privilege of having a victoria in summer in place of the sledge and at all times a landau in place of the coupe as you may desire. This is 50 rubles more than I pay, but the horses and indeed the entire turnout is very much better than mine. In any case, you can change if you are not satisfied.

Very faithfully yours,

Herbert H. D. Peirce

Peirce's letter, sent by diplomatic packet, reached Charlemagne just as he was leaving Vienna for Russia, a two-day, two-night journey by train. On his arrival, he stayed at the Grand Hotel d'Europa on the Rue Michel in St. Petersburg where he planned to stay until he found a house to lease.

Charlemagne's presentation to Tsar Nicholas II and the Tsarina took place at the Winter Palace on March 2, 1899. The American legation arrived in three carriages, each attended by two footmen, a coachman and a postilion rider mounted on the left front horse. The coach doors flashed with the gold and blue Imperial insignia. Mounted police escorted the cortege along the Nevski and through the archway into the large palace square. Charlemagne alighted first from his satin-lined carriage.

Herbert Hagerman, riding in the last carriage, recalled the scene when they entered the Winter Palace:

> On either side of the...hall was a row of big lackeys as stiff and still as the marble columns between which they stood. We proceeded up the Ambassador's marble staircase...and into a large room on one side of which was a squad of

---

2.   In 1899, two gold rubles equaled one dollar.

Chevalier's Gardes who all drew their big sabers with a great clash, extended them in the air and saluted.[3]

Far away in Vienna, Nellie, assisted by her sister, Gertrude, who was visiting from California, supervised the closing of the embassy residence and the packing of things to be shipped to St. Petersburg. Nellie knew that she would miss the beautiful little palace with its tropical garden under glass.

At the American Embassy in St. Petersburg, Herbert Hagerman was due to go on a six weeks leave, or *congé*, which he planned to spend in Vienna. Charlemagne gave him a letter of introduction to Samuel Clemens whom the Towers had been urging to visit them in St. Petersburg.

When Hagerman returned to Russia he reported that Mr. Clemens had told him with comic exaggeration that he would not be able to go to St. Petersburg because his family had gotten so irritated with him when they were all in Budapest that they refused to travel as far as Russia with him. This was all because Clemens got cross at his wife's German maid because she had not put his sleeve buttons and studs in his shirt one morning. To make matters worse, the same morning a package arrived from his publishers containing a thousand title pages to a deluxe edition of the *Tramp Abroad* for him to sign. He was there for fun, not to sign deluxe editions. When Hagerman had suggested that the family would no doubt feel differently soon, Clemens agreed that they certainly should, especially since he had gone around the world in thirteen months with them and always bottled up his temper until that shirt incident.[4]

In the spring of 1899, the diplomatic community in St. Petersburg was poised for news of the birth of the Empress's baby, due in May. The royal couple had two daughters and expectations were high that the baby would be a boy. The arrival of an heir to the throne would occasion celebrations at Court which would continue for weeks on end. As the Towers' guest, Gertrude would be part of the festivities.

But the baby was another girl. The birth of the infant Grand Duchess Marie Nicolaievna was an intense disappointment to the Russian people who had been in a frenzy of anticipation awaiting the birth. They blamed the German-born Empress Alexandra personally for not producing an heir.

While Nellie and Gertrude completed the final stages of packing in Vienna, Nellie sent the children with Hester and George and a nursemaid to stay at the Tischler Hotel in the mountain town of Znain on the Austrian-Czech border,

3.   Hagerman, 98.
4.   Ibid., 102.

famous for its magnificent scenery. Nellie and her sister Gertrude would join them as soon as the packing was complete.

In June, when a house still could not been found, and Nellie's presence was required in St. Petersburg to attend official functions, Nellie sent the children to England with Hester and George for the summer. Hester rented a cottage next door to her parents in the village of Balsham, in Cambridgeshire.

Nellie and Gertrude joined Charlemagne in St. Petersburg at the Hotel d'Europa. Nellie's official duties started immediately; in late June, she was presented first to the Empress Marie Fedorovna, the Tsar's mother, and then to Alexandra. A newspaper clipping from the *Gazette*, Elmira, New York, of June 29, 1899, gave a description of her costume for her presentation to the Tsarina Alexandra:

> Mrs. Charlemagne Tower, wife of the American Ambassador in St. Petersburg (formerly Minister in Vienna), was presented to the Tsarina a short time ago. The dress which she wore is of dove gray *crepe de chine*, with applications of real lace and pearl pailettes on the overdress, with ruches and flounces of the same material on the underdress, the vole made over gray silk. The high bodice is slightly draped, and has an empiecement of real lace, decorated with the tiniest of lavender ribbons, and finished off at the neck and waist with folds of lavender silk…Mrs. Tower is one of the most beautifully gowned women at the Russian court.

On Sunday July 9, Nellie and Charlemagne attended the baptism of the new baby, Grand Duchess Marie Nicolaievna, at the church of the Peterhof Palace.

Hester, George and the children had arrived in Balsham, England two weeks earlier. Nellie had arranged for the purchase of farm animals to amuse the children; Hester reported to on June 23:

> Father had the pig for Geoffrey, two white ducks for Dominie and a rabbit and chicken for Roderick, Helen and Baby. I wish you could have seen the children rush around. They are so happy here with Mother; if you should be delayed in Russia…you can be perfectly happy about the children.

Hester furnished the cottage economically, sending Nellie a full accounting of even the smallest purchase. On June 25, Hester reported that the children had completely settled into life in the country:

> They are allowed to do exactly as they like, and I wish you could hear Roderick talking to Father…Dominie spends all of his time with his ducks and has

contrived a most ingenious method of watering them. I really believe Geoffrey's pig is beginning to know him. Mother lets him feed it when he likes. Helen has an old wooden box in which she bathes her dolls and is as happy as a queen. The baby…plays around and amuses herself with any trifle…I am going to get the boys gardening tools and some kind of wagon to pull around. Then I shall get a few toys for the little girls…Our landlord who lives next door has a farm just outside of our back door. He is an old bachelor and is so pleased with the boys. They amuse him so much that he took them around to see the animals. They were charmed. One family of baby pigs greatly excited their admiration…Geoffrey's pig now knows him…Roderick put a whole bottle of water in with his rabbit in case it should get thirsty and the tiniest little cup beside it…

We had a beautiful leg of mutton with a pudding baked under it, new potatoes and green peas out of our garden. Then Mother made a jam pudding…

I often think that no king or queen can have the perfect happiness that we enjoy…When I look at the dear boys and the precious wee girlies I am rejoiced that they had a little taste of this country life, for they are growing so rapidly that the time will so soon come when they must take their places in this world's race.

Hester's letters must have brought tears of joy and longing to Nellie. She had never been away from her children for so long, or at such a great distance. She never doubted that her place was with her husband, carrying out her diplomatic duties as expected, but this resolve was not without aching homesickness for her children, especially her two daughters who were still so young.

In St. Petersburg, the Towers' search for a house had become a complete frustration, almost eclipsing the beauties of the Russian capital in summer. It was clear that there was nothing like the fine Springer Palace they had enjoyed in Vienna. The staff of the American Embassy were convinced that the Russians were making it difficult for the Towers to find a house in order to force the ambassador, or the United States government, to buy a residence, as no diplomat had ever had such a difficult time finding a house. Charlemagne was thoroughly disgusted.

In August, Nellie and Charlemagne decided to rent the von Devries house after all. It was not as large as they would have liked, it needed considerable work and the rent was very high, but it would have to do. They needed a home in which they could once again be together as a family and where they could start the official entertaining expected of foreign embassies.

Day-to-day business at the Embassy concerned issues large and small. Prominent Americans expected to be entertained at the Embassy; American businessmen requested introductions to Russian officials. American companies were well represented in the Russian economy, for instance Westinghouse made air brakes for the Siberian Railway and Russia imported many American-made products including farm machinery such as harvesters, reapers and plows.

Doing business in Russia could be difficult for American companies as there was a strong anti-American feeling in some quarters; disgruntled American businessmen would turn to the Embassy for help.

Under pressure from the Imperial Court, Charlemagne was forced to settle a matter of protocol that seems trivial by today's standards—what American diplomats should wear on formal occasions. Traditionally, they had always worn a black dress suit, but the Imperial Court felt this was too plain. Second Secretary Hagerman, too, found the prescribed black suit a problem: "We have always chased around by day and by night to any ball, baptism or funeral in dress suits, the only black crows in an aggregation of birds of paradise..." [5]

The Russian Imperial Court wanted the American legation to wear more elaborate clothes at formal occasions; they suggested a court costume like that of the British legation—a velvet jacket and knee breeches. Charlemagne refused to consider it because many ceremonies were held outdoors, even in the middle of winter. Instead, he designed a court uniform for the American legation of dark blue wool with gold embroidery on the shoulders and lapels, worn with a ceremonial sword and plumed hat.

Not all of the diplomatic problems were trivial, by any means. Since his arrival in St. Petersburg, Charlemagne had pressed the Russian government to settle the claims against Russia resulting from the seizure of American sealing vessels in the Bering Sea. In October 1899, Russia finally agreed, after eight years, to submit the claims to arbitration. The *New York Tribune*, Oct. 25, 1899, reported:

> This action [on the part of the Russians] is a source of great satisfaction to the United States Ambassador to Russia, Charlemagne Tower...He said today: "The relations between Russia and the United States were never more close or friendly than to-day. The only difference existing between the two nations is now sure of settlement on lines similar to the Venezuelan arbitration..."

By early November 1899, Nellie had settled her family into the newly redecorated von Devries house. She had augmented the house's furnishings with her own ornaments, pictures and carpets. The first formal dinner was a celebration of the American Thanksgiving, with a traditional American menu created by the

5.   Ibid., 106–107.

French chef. Fires blazed in every fireplace and jardinières of flowering plants brightened dark corners.

In Russia the Christmas season was celebrated by the European and American embassies on December 25, but in the Russian calendar, Christmas and New Year's were two weeks later. For the diplomatic community, observing both holidays made the Christmas season stretch a month or more.

Every day St. Petersburg was alive with the sound of church bells ringing throughout the city, dominated by the booming sound of those at Saint Isaac's Cathedral.

Presiding over the Russian Imperial Court at St. Petersburg in 1899 was the strikingly handsome young couple, the Tsar Nicholas II, age thirty-two, in the sixth year of his reign, and his beautiful twenty-eight year old wife, the Tsarina Alexandra.

Hagerman gave this description of the Tsar at a Cercle Diplomatic (a diplomatic reception):

> He has a very sympathetic face with keen, rather fascinating blue eyes and slightly turned up nose which gives him a young look. He is blond, his hair and beard quite light and thick. He frequently strokes his moustache when thinking of what to say or just before passing on to the next diplomat. There is a very amused, pleased and kindly twinkle in his eye and one could see him taking things in very thoroughly.[6]

Empress Alexandra Fedorouvna, born Princess Alix of Hesse-Darmstadt, was a granddaughter of Queen Victoria and a first cousin of Kaiser Wilhelm of Germany. She adored her husband and children, tolerated Court life, and tried to avoid confrontations with her mother-in-law, the Dowager Empress Marie, widow of Tsar Alexander III. She knew she was not popular with the Russian people, and yet she cared for them deeply. Famous for her exquisite needlework, she regularly donated finished pieces to be auctioned to help support several hospitals in the Crimea.

Nicholas felt at home anywhere in his vast Empire. In winter he and the Empress could be seen dashing around the snow-covered streets of St. Petersburg in an open sleigh pulled by a team of horses with the Tsar at the reins, and no bodyguard on board. The city police would be notified immediately and would keep track of royal couple as best they could, frantically telephoning ahead from

---

6.   Ibid., 79.

one precinct to another. Assassination was a constant threat which Nicholas chose to ignore.

At the Court in St. Peterburg, French was spoken rather than Russian. Invitations were in French, but dates were based on the Julian calendar which during the 1800's were twelve days behind the Gregorian calendar used by most European countries, and, starting in 1900, ran thirteen days behind.

The winter social season, simply known as The Season, began on New Year's Day and went non-stop until the beginning of Lent, with a succession of banquets, balls, ballets, opera (there were four opera houses in St. Petersburg), dinners and diplomatic receptions.

The Towers held their official embassy reception the first week in January 1900. The protocol for a diplomatic reception was strictly prescribed by the Court, with the guest list of two thousand invitations dictated by Court officials. Hagerman described the scene:

> Mrs. Tower had the hall and stairs well peopled with servants, the Switzer at the door, two flunkeys to pull the curtains, eight more in gala livery and powdered heads on the staircase, the chasseur with bandolier and sword at the top, then two creatures in solemn black to announce.
>
> They came straggling in at first, old generals hobbling along with difficulty, always the first to arrive, then Masters of the Court, Chamberlains, Equerries, Ambassadors, Grandes Maitresses, Demoiselles d'Honneur and all the rest...who move the Empire through the Tsar...It was interesting to see the highest in the Empire—The most haughty representatives of the world's one real autocracy [bowing to] us, American democrats, [emissaries] of the world's one real republic.[7]

The next week Ambassador Tower and secretaries Peirce and Hagerman attended the New Year's Day reception at the Winter Palace, which was held on January 13:

> The royal couple came in to us with the procession of grand dukes, functionaries and ministers, he attired in the white uniform of the Chevaliers Gardes, and she a perfect vision of beauty and magnificence in the Russian costume that well becomes her. It was of white satin bordered with sables...and nothing but diamonds, string after string covering her neck and bosom, and the kokoshnick or headdress of diamonds...He spoke some time and earnestly with the Ambassador...[8]

---

7.   Ibid., 140–141.
8.   Ibid., 192.

Charlemagne Tower, American Ambassador to
Russia, 1899–1902.
At the insistence of the Russian Court, Charlemagne designed this
uniform for official functions, in place of the black suit
American diplomats had previously worn.

Nellie Tower dressed to attend the Romanov Court,
St. Petersburg, Russia, 1900.

Nicholas II, Tsar of Russia, with the Empress Alexandra
1900.

The Ambassador's Staircase in the Winter Palace,
St. Petersburg, Russia.

The former palace of Grand Duke Vladimir in St. Petersburg, as it looks today. Situated on the Neva River a few blocks from the Winter Palace, it is directly across the river at the Citadel of St. Peter and St. Paul. The offices of the American Embassy occupied the third floor when Charlemagne Tower was the American Ambassador.

The horse-drawn sledge was a convenient way to travel around St.
Petersburg in winter.
In this picture, American Ambassador Charlemagne Tower wore a traditional fur coat, called a *chenell*. The large collar could be turned up past
the top of the hat.
A fur robe covered his lap and his feet were covered
with a large fur muff on the floor. March, 1899.

15

St. Petersburg 1900–1902

In May 1900, Nellie and the children left Russia to spend the summer in France. The Towers had rented the Chateau de Mesley at Tours where Nellie would stay with the children until he joined them later on his official leave. Then he and Nellie would travel together, leaving the children at the chateau with Hester and a small staff.

Nellie described the summer arrangements in a letter to her cousin, Emily Potter, written on Nov. 25, 1900:

> Our country home in France was a most successful undertaking. The children had all the pets they could think of and large grounds where they could ride their wheels or pony without leaving the Park.
> Taking it all in all, it was one of the happiest summers I ever had. The children are making splendid progress in every way and on my return to America, I shall be indeed very proud to have you meet them again.

Later in the summer, the letter continued, Nellie and Charlemagne spent two weeks in Paris visiting the Exposition which "…was a delight to us, but of course colossal and exceedingly difficult for ordinary sightseers to visit thoroughly, especially as we had at the same time a great amount of social duties."

They then went on to Spain. Writing to her sister, Gertrude, Nellie extolled the beauties of the Alhambra, the great Moorish castle in Granada. Nellie and Charlemagne traveled by train, with stays in Seville and Madrid before returning to Tours. Nellie was a tireless and attentive traveler who made notes on her observations.

She wrote Gertrude that she loved everything about Spain except the suffering of the poor, and the bullfights that she considered "degrading, brutal and barbarous."

In August, Nellie stayed on in Tours with the children and Charlemagne returned to America, where he met with President McKinley at the President's summer home in Canton, New York, near the Canadian border. As soon as Charlemagne returned to Atlantic City, New Jersey, he wrote his wife about the visit, addressing her by the pet name, "Nennie."

> Friday, August 3, 1900
> My dear Nennie,
>
> I have had a wonderful day with the President. It will be impossible for me to narrate it to you now, but I shall tell you all about its most interesting details when I see you, which I hope to do soon...
>
> When my train arrived in Canton, the President's carriage was at the station and I went directly to his house. He was waiting for me and received me with the greatest cordiality—thanking me at once for having come. He inquired for you and so did Mrs. McKinley, who was there also, and both send you many kind messages. The President asked all about your surroundings in France, and the children, and your plans for the summer with evident interest. He placed me at once upon a footing of easy comradeship that made me feel comfortable, which evidently was his intention.
>
> Senator Fairbanks of Indiana was there and we all took a drive in the President's carriage...we had the most delightful conversation which drifted back and forth to Russia and America and then to politics or personal subjects or general topics, as the impulse directed it.
>
> After lunch with Mrs. McKinley and the President's Secretary, the President took me into the library and, closing the door, we sat there for two hours, during which I talked to him with the utmost freedom upon European questions, giving him full replies to his many inquiries...It left me with the impression afterwards of having come into as close and intimate contact with President McKinley as his trusted advisers, and it established a personal friendship between him and me that I could not have hoped for. He said, "Mr. Tower, you have the most important post, next to London, in the American service," and he added, "You must know how gratified I am with the way in which you have conducted it."

Charlemagne sailed for Europe on August 8 on *The Deutschland* and joined Nellie and the children for a holiday at St. Malo, France, on the coast of Brittany.

In late fall Nellie and the children spent several weeks in Germany en route back to Russia. Charlemagne wrote from St. Petersburg to his eleven-year-old son, Dominie, at the Hotel Kaiserhof in Wiesbaden on November 26, 1900: "We have a little snow in St. Petersburg every day, so that the ground is white but there is no sleighing yet. The Neva is still open though ice was flowing in it yesterday. Our house is all ready, waiting for Mamma to come back with all of you boys and girls, a week from today."

January and February of 1901 were filled with receptions and formal dinners. The first of two imperial balls, called the Big Ball, was for those in the first four classes of society. Four thousand invitations were issued and an estimated 3,600 guests sat down to supper in the three enormous chambers at the top of the Ambassador's staircase, Salle Alexandra II, Salle Nicholas I and Salle des Concerts. From Hagerman's eye witness account:[1]

> In the great room of Nicholas I where the…guests were nearly all assembled…the orchestra bursts into beautiful music, the great doors open and the Empress, blazing with diamonds, appears with the Tsar, one feels that he is witnessing one of the most imposing spectacles of royal pageantry that remains in this practical age…the emperor, empress and grand dukes and duchesses have a walk around, hand in hand up and down the length of the room once…then they change partners and do it again…then all of the foreign diplomats are greeted.

The most elaborate was the Ball of the Palms that took place a week later, but for only 800 guests, almost intimate by Russian standards. Instead of full uniforms and decorations, men wore dress suits with brass buttons, a style of dress referred to as *boutons metaliques;* women wore ball gowns. Dancing was in the Salle des Concerts. At midnight the doors to the enormous Salle Nicholas I were thrown open and guests gasped in awe when they saw the room transformed into a tropical paradise with full size palm trees almost touching the ceiling. Arranged under the trees were flowering shrubs, spring bulbs and hundreds of small tables for dining. The Tsar strolled from one table to the next, having a word or two with various guests, before taking his seat with the Empress Alexandra at a raised dias for special dignitaries.

In spring of 1901 it was rumored that General Horace Porter, the American Ambassador to Paris, might be recalled to serve in President McKinley's administration, which would leave the prestigious American Embassy at Paris open. Rumors suggested that Charlemagne would take his place. Nothing would have pleased the Towers more.

Nellie and Charlemagne found the long, dark, Russian winters difficult and depressing. The bitter cold was confining for the children and caused Charlemagne to suffer from painful bouts of bronchitis. Winter started in late fall when huge blocks of ice flowed into the Neva River from Lake Ladoga. The blocks

---

1.   Hagerman, 144.

quickly froze into a mass of thick ice, over which roadways and pedestrian crossings were constructed to cross the river. Once the snow came, it usually lasted until May.

Added to the discomfort of the cold was the isolation of Russia. Visiting other European capitals from St. Petersburg required at least a two-day train ride. This made short visits to other countries impossible.

By the end of the long Russian winter, Nellie and the children longed for sunshine. In April, they left St. Petersburg for Tours, France, where they again took up residence at the Chateau de Mesley, where Charlemagne would join them later on. From France Nellie wrote her sister, Gertrude, on June 2, 1901, sharing some of her uncertainties about the future in St. Petersburg:

Chateau de Mesley

Rochecorbon
Indre-et-Loire
My darling Gretchie,

You who know so well the old history of travelling and getting established in the new home with its many demands can imagine perfectly well the fatigue and the duties I have had since leaving Russia. All has gone wonderfully well with us thus far and we are so well settled here that it seems as if it would be a lovely summer for the dear little people.

Our long journey from Russia was made with so much comfort and in such delightful weather that we were not even tired when we reached Paris. The pony and the dogs knew the children and they were in a state of ecstasy. The housekeeper—or rather the person who is to take charge here for me, for she is not in any sense a servant—is a charming person and I feel very proud of myself for having made this selection.

Madame Limonot is so thoughtful and painstaking, and weighs the provisions and looks after everthing with a care and watchfulness that I never understood. The children have always loved her and her influence over the boys is most helpful—at the same time, she is companionable to me when the little ones are asleep. Then, too, I am having constant practice in speaking the best of French and her regular lessons with the boys give them duties enough to make them love their play.

The country looks so lovely after the long winter in Russia that I want to play all day long.

I am negotiating for two ponies for Dominie and Geoffrey to ride or drive—a donkey for the little girls with a basket phaeton and for Roderick a pair of goats with a cart—this latter is a perfect success. With all these means of locomotion and for myself a Victoria and one horse, we shall be well off and yet not living extravagantly.

The boys have commenced tumbling again in the pond, but as it is not very deep it is not serious—you know how they love floating the boats! On Wednesday I take the maid and go to Paris, from there to London to join Charlemagne en route for Glasgow. We have been invited to visit, while there, at a charming house and I am looking forward to it all with untold pleasure—I think the whole thing will be so refreshing in many ways.

After our trip there, I have no possible idea what we shall do. I may go back to Russia with Charlemagne or I may come here to the children. The Tsar's oldest child is ill, they say with typhoid fever—if it proved to be so then there will be no fetes of any kind not even if an heir is born—thus we are planning nothing. We cannot. It is a great problem to me because I have to take all my baggage about with me everywhere—even to Scotland, where I may need one dress or perhaps twenty. This is particularly embarrassing where one is visiting and must have the proper toilets and yet not wish to move in with one trunk larger than any you have ever yet seen, one smaller and two hat boxes. And yet what may be expected of me?

Of the plan to go to Paris in the event Charlemagne were named Ambassador, we hear absolutely nothing and I fear there has been a complete change in former plans. That seems absolutely dead—dead without any hope of living again and you can imagine our disappointment, also the impossibility of knowing what we may or may not do next winter...

My desk is a mass of flowers which the children have brought me and I thoroughly enjoy it. Today we all walked and had such a happy time. Dear little Gertrude always keeps tight hold of one hand and I carry her at the slightest excuse for the sake of having her loving arms about me—

Charlemagne's sister Emma and her daughter Ruth expect to come over next September to spend the winter in Europe—happily for us they never even heard of our possibly going to Paris—or at least they never mentioned it...

Good night my darling. I will write you from England—please send this on to Adie because I cannot write again before leaving and yet I think of you all so constantly...

Ever your devoted,
Nenno

By the summer of 1901, Charlemagne was most anxious to leave Russia. His mentors in Philadelphia and Washington were at work on his behalf and influential friends contacted the President.

Joseph Wharton, the Pennsylvania industrialist and philanthropist, wrote to President McKinley on Charlemagne's behalf on August 6, 1901, praising the Ambassador's "solidity of character, his habit of punctual attention to business, his intelligent sympathy with the policy of your administration, his command of the principal European languages, his candid demeanor and knowledge of etiquette..."

What President McKinley intended for Charlemagne's next post we do not know. While attending a Pan American Exposition in Buffalo, New York, on September 6, 1901, the President was assassinated by an anarchist. He died a week later, leaving the country shocked and saddened. Vice-President Theodore Roosevelt became president.

Charlemagne and his staff arranged a memorial service for the late president at the British-American Church in St. Petersburg. On September 10, Charlemagne wrote Nellie who was still in France with the children: "The memorial services...were impressive, the singing excellent...A large congregation filled the church...Of all the ceremonies I have had to go through in official life, this was the most painful and trying. I am glad I was at my post to fulfill my duty..."

Nothing could be decided about a new post for Charlemagne until President Theodore Roosevelt had settled into the presidency and had time to address the matter. Charlemagne carried on in his post as American Ambassador to Russia.

In the fall of 1901, Dominie was twelve, Geoffrey, eleven and Roderick, nine. Schooling for them in Russia had become a problem. Nellie and Charlemagne were no longer satisfied with tutors and whatever international schools existed in St. Petersburg at the time. The boys' command of French and German was often better than their English, which would not be acceptable when they returned to American schools. They also needed to be with other boys their own ages for sports and camaraderie.

The Towers decided to send the three boys to The Villa School in Lausanne, Switzerland, in the fall of 1901, to begin their preparation for boarding school in the United States, possibly the following year.

To help them acclimate gradually to being on their own, Nellie and the little girls and their governess stayed at the Hotel Gibban in Lausanne where the boys joined them on the weekends. In December, Nellie and the children returned to St. Petersburg for the holidays and for the festive post-Christmas season. Then the boys returned to Switzerland for school on their own.

In January, the Towers gave a dinner in honor of General Horace Porter, American Ambassador to France and Mrs. Porter to which they invited high Russian officials and members of the diplomatic community as well as Charlemagne's sister Emma and her daughter, Ruth.

The *New York Herald* reported the event on January 30, 1902: "After dinner a concert was given in the music room of the Embassy...which was attended by a couple of hundred guests…Dancing began later,and was continued with great animation and brilliancy until long after midnight."

The following evening, Tuesday, January 21, the Towers presented the Porters and the Reillys to the Emperor and Empress at the Court Ball at the Winter Palace, for which three thousand invitations were issued. The women's gowns on these occasions were elaborate and costly. *The New York Times* reported on the event in February 1902:

> Mrs. Tower wore cloth of gold, with trimmings of Venetian lace and a train of pale pink and green brocade embroidered with gold…Mrs. Thomas Alexander Reilly wore white brocade, embroidered with silver. Miss Snyder looked exceedingly well in white satin, with pink roses and silver embroidery.
>
> During the first quadrille, Ambassador Tower had for his partner the Grand Duchess Sergius. Opposite them were the Tsarina and Sir Charles Scott [the British Ambassador].
>
> The guests dined in the great Gerbovoi Zaal. [Hall of Coats of Arms]. The Tsarina sat on a dais, surrounded by ranking representatives of the Diplomatic Corps…The Tsar, as is the Russian custom, passed from table to table, greeting and chatting with the guests…

In April, during the boys' spring vacation from school, Nellie took all the children to Villeneuve, Switzerland, on Lake Geneva. Geoffrey wrote to a friend on April 1, 1902, describing the two-week holiday: The little girls "have their dogs and are very happy…Mama is going to have a party next Friday and she is going to invite some of the Americans of the school."

In May, Nellie and Charlemagne went to London to attend a reception at the court of King Edward VII, held on May 3 at Buckingham Palace. They had arranged for Charlemagne's sister, Emma Reilly, and her daughter, Ruth Snyder, to be presented to the King and Queen. For young, unmarried American girls, being presented at the English court was the ultimate social distinction. Nellie took pleasure in securing invitations to these dazzling occasions for the daughters of family and friends.

On this evening, she was also shepherding Letitia Ellicott Wright, whose mother was a close friend from Philadelphia. Letitia's younger sister, Annette, too young to attend the ball, remembered her sister, "trying on a most beautiful gown, with a long train, in which she was to be presented at the court of King Edward VII, while visiting Mr. and Mrs. Tower who were staying in London. It was a time of peace. Queen Victoria's children were the crowned heads, or were married to the crowned heads, of many European countries. There were balls and parties of all kinds in the grand style and my sister had an exciting and wonderful time…"[2]

The engraved invitation to the ball included the enchanting phrase, "Ladies with Feathers and Trains," to describe the approved dress for the evening. The *New York Herald*, Paris edition, on May 3, 1902, provided this picturesque account:

A ROYAL COURT
King Edward and Queen Alexandra
Hold the Second Function of the Season

London, Saturday—The King and Queen held their second Court at Buckingham Palace last night. The attendance was very numerous. The scene in the Palace was one of great splendor. Down the Mall and Constitution Hill, soon after nine o'clock, carriages poured in an endless stream. Behind the slowly rumbling town coach of some ancient family with its gorgeous footmen behind, would be an automobile, its levers shining in the gaslight, throbbing and chafing with the delay, and next perhaps, a modest, little, one-horse brougham.

The fine ballroom on the first floor, which is now used as the Throne Room, was ablaze with light and beautifully decorated with palms and flowers. The King, with Her Majesty on his left, the Lord Chamberlain on his right, took up his position at the upper end of the room at ten o'clock, the members of the Royal Family standing in a group behind the Queen, who wore an ivory satin dress, embroidered with gold, with a train of rich brocade and cloth of gold…She wore a magnificent tiara of diamonds, ropes of pearls and diamond ornaments on the bodice of her dress, which was a blaze of precious stones…

Mrs. Charlemagne Tower wore yellow satin, richly embroidered with gold, and a train of pale blue satin embroidered with gold and yellow floss. Mrs. Tower's jewels were diamonds and pearls.

---

2. Annette Wright Wood's description comes from a letter written by her to a Tower cousin, Alfred Putnam, in 1973.

St. Petersburg, Russia 1900.
Gertrude, Nellie and Helen

St. Petersburg, Russia, 1900.
From left, Roderick, Charlemagne, Geoffrey and Dominie.

Charlemagne Tower's sister, Emma Reilly, and her
daughter, Ruth, dressed in "feathers and trains," the
prescribed costume for ladies being presented at the
Court of St. James in England. As guests of the Towers,
they attended King Edward VIII's second court
reception, London, May 3, 1902.

By early summer, it was a certainty that Charlemagne would be named Ambassador to Germany; he would assume the post in January of 1903. Charlemagne had now reached the ultimate diplomatic assignment, an ambassadorship in one of the three major diplomatic posts—Berlin, London, or Paris. He had every right to be proud of his accomplishment.

It was now definite that the Tower boys would be leaving for school in the United States in the fall of 1902, where they would attend the Fay School in Southborough, Massachusetts. It was a painful decision for their parents, but one they felt was necessary for the good of the boys.

Nellie would accompany them to the United States and settle them in school. She and the boys stayed at Garlant's Hotel in London, awaiting their departure for the United States. Dominie wrote to his father at St. Petersburg:

> Garlants Hotel, London, September 2, 1902
> Dear Papa,
>   I expect this is the last letter that you will receive from me until I get to America.
>   It seems a sad thing, but I understand why it is necessary, and I know it _is_ necessary, that we should go to school and learn something...
>   It has been raining in London today, and the weather has been very disagreeable. Mrs. Russell, the wife of Governor Russell from Massachusetts (who is now dead) is coming to take dinner with us tonight. I will send you an account of the school when I get there.
>   I always remain your affectionate son:
>   Charlemagne Tower, Jr.

Nellie, Dominie, Geoffrey and Roderick sailed for the United States in September. They went directly to Southborough where Nellie settled them in to their new school. However much she liked the school, it was still heartrending to leave the boys, knowing that she would not see them again for eight months.

Before sailing for Europe, Nellie spent a few days in Philadelphia where she was quoted in the September 29, 1902 issue of _The American,_ about the decision to send the boys to school in the United States. "It is not that foreign schools are inadequate," she told a reporter, "but because we felt that the boys should grow up to be loyal Americans, and that therefore they should go to school in this country."

From St. Petersburg, Charlemagne wrote Nellie a letter of great compassion which she received just before she was due to leave for her return voyage:

Wednesday, 17 September 1902
My dear Nennie,

I have been thinking of you all, yesterday and today, as probably having gone to Southborough to see the place and of the boys as making their entry at Mr. Fay's today. Therefore, your telegram which came this morning, has made me most happy, especially because you say that you are delighted with the school and have taken your passage on *The Majestic* for October 1st.

You have now done your work and done it well. How anxious I shall be to hear all about it from you when you get back! It has been a wonderful undertaking, and it has been one that called for rare courage on your part. The best of it now is...that the school is equal to your expectations. It has been the hardest task of your life, Nennie; and how wonderfully you have accomplished it, with all credit to yourself and gratification to me. Now come back!...

There is nothing new here—The time is terribly long. It requires all my self-control to face it from day to day, but when you come all will be right.

GoodBye, Nennie, a safe voyage to you—

Your affectionate Husband,
Charlemagne Tower

The retiring American Ambassador in Berlin, Andrew D. White, wrote to Charlemagne at St. Petersburg on September 26, 1902, offering congratulations on his appointment:

My dear colleague:

...I trust that you will allow me to congratulate you as well as Mrs. Tower, and to express the earnest hope and belief that your duties will meet the same acknowledged success in this new post as at those you have already held, and that to both Mrs. Tower and yourself the life here will prove interesting and agreeable...

As to a house, you will probably be more fortunate than I was. When I came, my wife and I were obliged to hunt for weeks, and found nothing save one first-floor apartment, two miles out from the diplomatic quarter, and a second-floor apartment, very beautiful and commodious, in the diplomatic quarter. This I was obliged to take, refit with electricity and water, renew the floors and decorate the walls of the main apartments and furnish it completely. It was impossible to furnish it to any extent in Berlin, and we were obliged to go to Dresden, London and Paris for the purpose, sending furniture, etc., in...wagons with upholsterers, artisans, etc., from the latter city; and even then, though we had several months, I was obliged to drive out the artisans only five minutes before the arrival of the Chancellor, Prince Hohenlohe, at the first of my three official receptions.

I hope that you may be more fortunate...

Reading White's letter, Charlemagne must have recalled with some bitterness how difficult the Russians had made it for him to find a house in St. Petersburg. Surely, Berlin would be an improvement.

That fall Charlemagne continued at his post as American Ambassador in St. Petersburg. He and Nellie had moved out of the von Devries house when the lease ended at the end of October; they were again staying at the Hotel d'Europa. Charlemagne could not leave until the Tsar returned to St. Petersburg from the Crimea where he was vacationing with his family. Then Charlemagne could attend the formal leave-taking reception which protocol required.

To the surprise of the diplomatic community, the Tsar broke with a long-standing tradition and invited Charlemagne and Nellie to visit him at Livadia, the royal palace in the Crimea. The Towers would make the trip in November; Prince Hilkoff, Minister of Ways and Communications, would order a special railroad car to be attached to the Sebastopol Express train for them.

The Crimea, on the shores of the Black Sea, has lush vegetation and a mild climate throughout the year. Before the Revolution, beautiful villas belonging to the royal family and the aristocracy nestled in a royal preserve between the cliffs and the sea. For Nicholas and Alexandra, their palace at Livadia was one of their favorite places.[3]

Nellie returned from America the first week in October. This letter to Dominie is undated:

> My dear Dominie,
>
> What a delightful letter Papa had from you yesterday and I received one from dear Geoffrey.
>
> You are both so happy at the school and little Roderick too that now we feel sure, do we not dear boys, that the great sacrifice we have all made is for your good?
>
> How hard it was for us to decide to do it but how certain we now are that it is for the best. Now that everything is going so well with you all, I am very happy to be going to Berlin and I think it is a great thing for your father. America and Germany seem equally pleased at the appointment and all the newspapers in both countries speak most flattering of his ability and splendid reputation.
>
> The Tsar of Russia has sent him word he is to go to the Crimea to see him to say farewell and this is a favor which has never been shown before to any ambassador from any government or country. We are to have a private railroad car quite to ourselves to make that long journey and every attention shown to us while we are there. Does not this make you <u>very</u> proud of your

---

3.   Massie, *Nicholas and Alexandra,* 162.

father? The weather here now is very cold, but clear and bright—the river is beginning to freeze over…give a great deal of love to Geoffrey and Roderick and for yourself, my dear, dear Dominie, accept a whole heartfull.

Your devoted mother,
Helen S.Tower

Charlemagne wrote to Dominie giving him this detailed account of the historic trip to the Crimea:

Sebastopol
November 21, 1902,
My dear Dominie,

This is a long way off and it will probably take my letter longer to reach you from here than if I waited for a day or two and wrote to you from Vienna, for instance, where we expect to be early next week, or from Paris; but I send it from here because Mamma and I are just about to leave Russia, this being our last stopping place and because of the interest you will take some day in the fact that you have had a letter from Sebastopol, especially when you are a little older and come to read of the Crimean War during which the siege took place that has made this city famous in the world.

Mamma and I came here from St. Petersburg last week. It took us three nights and two days to make the railway journey, but as Prince Hilkoff, who has charge of the railways in Russia, had given us a car of our own to travel in, we were not uncomfortable. The car was quite like the ones we all had last summer in Switzerland, you remember, to go to Interlaken, only that it was much larger. Mamma had a sleeping room and a bathroom whilst I had a good-sized room to myself. There was a large sitting room in which we took our meals. Besides this there were places for Otto who is with us and Marie, Mamma's maid; in addition to the Conductor who waited upon us as well as a man whose duty it was to look after the electric lights.

So, with all this we succeeded in getting along very well.

After staying one day in Sabastopol, we took a carriage to Yalta, where the Emperor lives at present; you know the cause of our coming to the Crimea is to say farewell to him and the Empress before we go away from Russia to join our new post at Berlin.

This drive to Yalta, which takes from about eight o'clock in the morning until six at night, along a beautiful road, very smooth and well kept and running most of the time directly along the shore of the Black Sea. We spent three days in Yalta and then came back here again by carriage today. Yalta is one of the most beautiful places in Russia besides being the favorite seaside resort of the people of the Empire. Its many pretty villas looking out over the sea recall Newport in the attractiveness of their situation. It is in one of these villas, called <u>Livadia,</u> that the Emperor spends a part of each autumn, and he is fond of coming to it because here he can escape the formality of the Court at St. Petersburg and rest from his great cares.

Mamma and I found him living quite like a country gentleman and he and the Empress invited us to luncheon as soon as they knew that we had arrived. We enjoyed our visit very greatly. For, although there were perhaps thirty people at table, ladies and gentlemen of the household and high officers at the Court, Mamma sat by the Emperor and I by the Empress so that we had a good opportunity to talk with them. And when we came away they invited us to return to Russia if ever we had an opportunity, which we promised to do.

Tomorrow morning we shall go back to our car and travel...two days more, to the frontier of Austria whence another days' ride takes us to Vienna. We intend to stop there for only a single day on our way to Paris. Of this, both Mamma and I shall write you hereafter. We send our love to all of you.

Your affectionate Father, Charlemagne Tower

The landmark train trip to Yalta had a profound affect on Charlemagne, so well expressed in the letter to Dominie. Charlemagne recorded his bittersweet reflections on his time in Russia. He may have written them on the long train ride from Yalta to Vienna en route to Paris We do not know whether he intended them for a memoir, a diary entry or perhaps a report to the State Department. He compared Emperor Franz Joseph, Tsar Nicholas II and Kaiser Wilhelm—

> Three men of the same position but different surrounds and influences...with a consequent difference in personality...3 great Empires—the autocratic bureaucracy—the aristocratic oligarchy—and the modern government based upon enlightenment and science...
>
> The life of each sovereign is influenced by his own traditions and surroundings...Whilst all are withdrawn from public contact and each is inaccessible, the Emperor of Russia leads the most isolated life. He is the "Little Father,"...a man of kindly nature, wishing only the good of his people...but limited in his ability to do for them by the character of the bureaucratic system which cannot be changed without upsetting the whole fabric of government...He persists in efforts to help the welfare of the people...

Of the Russian people themselves, Charlemagne made note of "The progress of the people...their intelligence...and their dependence on vodka, The People's Palace."

In contrast to all of this, he noted, was

> The splendor of the Court and the wealth of the nobility...The Ball of the Palms at which I danced with the Empress and glimpsed her sweetness...how the life of the Emperor and Empress at the Winter Palace was bound by endless ceremonies played out against a constant danger of assassination...the Emperor with his punctilious attention to official duties...and ceremonies...the blessing of the Neva, The New Years Reception, the launching of ships and all religious ceremonies.
>
> Church services...endlessly long but graced with magnificent music...My own approach to the Tsar and...the Reception by the Emperor and Empress...and the formality which nothing pierces.

American diplomats could not accept honors from a foreign government while in the service of the State Department. Charlemagne accepted two high honors in the interim period between retiring as Ambassador to Russia and becoming Ambassador to Germany.

The Tsar conferred on him the Grand Cordon of the Saint Alexander Nevsky Order, and the French government awarded him the Legion of Honor in appreciation for his two-volume book, *The Marquis de La Fayette in the American Revolution.*

Charlemagne's achievements while Ambassador to Russia, assessed by John E. Findling in American Diplomatic History, included the arbitration agreement by which the Russians finally made restitution for seizing American sealing in the Bering Sea. Also of note was "advocacy of the Open Door Policy for Manchuria, where Russian influence was strong."

Passport picture of the Tower boys in 1902
when they left St. Petersburg to attend school in the
United States. Geoffrey, at left, was 12, Dominie was 13,
and Roderick was 10.

16

Berlin 1903–1904

Berlin was a different world from St. Petersburg, and one with which Nellie and Charlemagne were familiar. They both spoke German, and Charlemagne knew the capital well from his student days. A cosmopolitan city with a milder winter climate was a welcome change.

Nellie and Charlemagne spent Christmas in Paris, then at the end of December moved to the Hotel de Roma in Berlin, to begin the search for a house.

The official reception for new ambassadors took place on January 2, 1903. Charlemagne described the Kaiser's distinct style in his book, *Essays Political and Historical*:[1]

> The German Emperor holds his audience at Potsdam or Berlin with great military state, surrounded by a brilliant staff of officers....He usually steps forward to greet the approaching diplomatist, who pronounces a few words of international greeting from his own country with the expression of hope, as he hands him his letter of credence, that the cordial relations may long continue to subsist between the two governments. Whereupon the Emperor in receiving the document makes an equally formal reply...
>
> That having been accomplished, the serious tone changes, and with an engaging smile the Kaiser enters into a personal conversation with his visitor, in a manner quite his own, full of manliness and high feeling, which has always won the cordial sympathy of those who have come into personal contact with him. In conversing with the American and British diplomatic representatives in Germany he speaks English, with which he is perfectly familiar and shows no trace of a foreign accent; though he uses French generally with envoys of other countries.

On January 20, 1903, Nellie and Charlemagne attended a luncheon given by Prince and Princess Henry of Prussia at Schloss Konigliche. Prince Henry was the Kaiser's younger brother; his wife, Irene of Hesse, was a sister of the Empress

---

1.   Tower, Charlemagne, *Essays Political and Historical*, 76

Alexandra of Russia. On February 11, the Towers attended a ball at the Schloss Konigliche.

After some weeks spent looking at houses in Berlin, Nellie and Charlemagne concluded that the best choice was the grand and well situated Pringheim Palace. Andrew D. White, the outgoing American Ambassador, described it as "the finest available house in Berlin for diplomatic purposes, one finer, more comfortable, more convenient and more stately than any of the existing Embassies, save the Russian and the French."[2]

The Pringheim Palace[3], at number 4 Koenigsplatz, was directly across a broad boulevard from the parliament building and to one side the beautiful city park, the Tiergarten. The Towers leased the premises, and began extensive renovations. The rent was a staggering $18,000 per year, $500 more than Charlemagne's annual salary as ambassador.

Thousands of miles away, the three Tower boys were enduring various stages of homesickness at the Fay School. In a letter to his father written on January 18, Dominie, the oldest and the most sensitive of the boys, lamented: "I often think of the days you used to read to us in Russia, Oh! The lovely times we used to have, will never come back again, no, never."

On Jan 30 Charlemagne replied to Dominie's letter and sought to focus the boy's longing on the summer when the family would be together again at the old Tower Homestead in Waterville, New York:

> My dear Dominie,
>   ...I am thinking as you are too, of the pleasure it will be to be united once more next summer. It is true, the delightful evenings of our home in Russia are gone forever; but I trust there are others in store for us in the future. Waterville is a little country village, but the summers there are most enjoyable and the generations of children and grandchildren who have spent them in the old Homestead for nearly a hundred years past have found great pleasure, so that I think you boys will do so too.

Dominie's spirits improved in March when he won prizes at the Fay School Field Day. He wrote to his father proudly, "My name will be put up on the record board and you can see it when you come."

---

2.   Letter from Andrew D. White to Charlemagne Tower dated September 26, 1902.

3.   The Pringheim Palace and the surrounding neighborhood was demolished by Hitler and his architect Albert Speer in the first phase of a massive rebuilding campaign to make Berlin the capital of a supra-German state—*Welthauptstadt Germania*.

On April 5 Charlemagne wrote to Dominie congratulating him on his awards and imparted some paternal advice:

> When I come to the school, I shall look for your name on the board. You will always think with pride of everything you do well, throughout your life; and so will Mamma and I.
>
> But remember, it is not enough to excel in one thing. There is the opportunity to make a record by studying well, by being a good boy, and after a while, by becoming a useful man. Let me have some statistics about these also.

The three boys spent a part of their spring vacation with Charlemagne's sister, Emma Reilly, in Philadelphia, and part with another sister, Grace Putnam, who also lived in Philadelphia at the time.

Nellie and Charlemagne moved into the Pringheim Palace in early March. The house had generous proportions. From a large front hall with a marble floor of black and white squares, a broad marble staircase led upstairs to a succession of five drawing rooms across the front of the house. The main drawing room was furnished with Louis XV pieces; the furniture in smaller chambers was Empire and Directoire. Nellie and Charlemagne held their first reception on April 4, for one thousand members of the court and the diplomatic community.

The Kaiser was actively pursuing a close relationship with America. He conceived of numerous gifts to send from Germany to the United States, all of which went through the American Embassy. Soon after his arrival, Charlemagne reported in a letter to his son, Dominie:

> The Emperor sent for me to go with him to see some beautiful plaster casts of statues and architecture that he is sending as a present to the art museum of Harvard University. Some time you and I shall see them together, in Cambridge, and I shall then point them out to you as he did to me.

The Kaiser took an immediate liking to Charlemagne, who spoke perfect German, had studied in Germany, traveled throughout the country and knew its history. An easy formality was established between the two men.

The Kaiser had commissioned a statue of his ancestor, Frederick the Great, as a gift to the American people. When completed, it would be placed on the grounds of the War College in Washington, D.C. *The New York Herald* of Jan. 2, 1903 reported:

The Kaiser was pleased that the statue would stand among other famous com-
manders who belonged to all the world and to all time and equally pleased
that Ambassador Tower could be at the unveiling. His Majesty said today that
the Ambassador's presence upon that occasion would be a compliment to
Germany...

The Kaiser would send a commission to accompany the statue and among
them would be descendants of German officers who had fought under Washington in the American Revolution.

On June 5, 1903, Charlemagne received a letter from Andrew Carnegie who
had decided to accept the Presentation Committee's invitation to be present at
the unveiling of the statue, scheduled to take place in Washington, D.C. that fall.
Charlemagne had become a friend of Carnegie's and the Towers had visited the
Carnegies the previous summer at Skibo Castle in Dornoch, Scotland.

The millionaire industrialist, then sixty-eight years old, was devoting all of his
considerable energies and a good deal of his fortune to large-scale philanthropic
projects including the cause of world peace. He considered Kaiser Wilhelm "the
most remarkable man living—power and ability combined," he told Charlemagne in the June 5 letter.

Carnegie's Temple of Peace in the Hague in Holland had been recently completed. It would house the Permanent Court of Arbitration, the International
Court of Justice, The Hague Academy of International Law and a library of
books on international law, which would be at the disposal of the Court of Arbitration. It was Carnegie's hope that solving disputes through the Court of Arbitration would help to maintain world peace. Carnegie wrote to Charlemagne on
June 14, 1903:

...I have received from Count Cassani, the Russian [Ambassador] in Washington, a very nice note this morning re. Hague Temple of Peace: "The
Emperor [Tsar Nicholas] directs [me] to convey the expression of his deep and
heartfelt appreciation of this magnificent gift [which will be] of inestimable
value to the future peace of the world and the happiness of the world..."

If you and I were the two Emperors [of Russia and Germany] now how
soon we should agree to the status quo and decide that no power in Europe
should draw the sword without finding us at hand to enforce peace—

These two men could perform this seeming miracle—at least you and I
could because we would grandly dare—do or die...

Nellie and her daughters, Helen and Gertrude, sailed for America on the *Kronz-
prinz Wilhelm*, and arrived in New York on June 6. Nellie would collect the three

boys from the Fay School and proceed to Waterville, New York, where they would all spend the summer in the Tower Homestead. The children would be seeing the old house for the first time. Hester Candler had gone on ahead to supervise the opening of the house. Charlemagne would join them there in mid-July.

When Nellie was reunited with the boys, she was alarmed to find that thirteen-year-old Geoffrey had lost weight, and was limping. She immediately consulted a doctor in Philadelphia whose diagnosis was tuberculosis of the hip joint. There was no medicine that could help; the doctor prescribed rest, warm sunshine, mild exercise and the use of a leg brace.

Geoffrey's condition was a grave concern. Tuberculosis at that time could be a death sentence. Charlemagne's grandfather, Reuben Tower, had struggled against the disease for years before succumbing to it at the age of forty-four.

Instead of going to Waterville, Nellie took Geoffrey to Atlantic City in hopes that the salt water and warm air would help him recuperate. Dominie, Roderick, Helen and Gertrude, stayed in Waterville with Hester and Bertha, and other members of the staff.

On June 18, Dominie wrote Geoffrey from Waterville: "I hope that you are feeling better since you have been at Atlantic City. Do not think I have forgotten you, because I have not. I think about you all the time, in fact all of us do."

At the end of June, Charlemagne went to Kiel, the German port on the Baltic Sea, for the Kaiser's annual Regatta. Regatta week at Kiel was like an international exposition and maritime display. Those seeking invitations made their requests through their respective embassies; the various embassies for their part were eager to have key figures from their countries attend. A good deal of international diplomacy took place at Kiel both at the races and afterwards at receptions and dinners.

Charlemagne wrote Nellie from Kiel on June 25, sharing his pleasure that things were going so well:

> My dear Nennie,
>   I am so much occupied, as you will very naturally understand, with the hundreds of claims that are made upon me here that I shall have to give you the detailed account of the incidents that are taking place, when I get home.
>   In the meantime, everything is going in the most gratifying manner possible.
>   The Emperor is here, the American ships make a fine showing and the weather is brilliant. No more could be done than is being done by everybody concerned to make the occasion both successful and memorable. Of course, you will know the principal details of it through the newspapers before this reaches you. But you will understand the rest of it when we are talking

together. I never wished so much that you could be with me. For this is the high water mark of my career, up to the present at all events...

I was invited to luncheon with Prince and Princess Henry the following day and have had invitations of the most agreeable kind; amongst them one from the Emperor to dine this evening on the *Hohenzollern* [the royal yacht]...

I hope we may all be there happily together before the summer is over—

Love to you all,

Your affectionate Husband,

Charlemagne Tower

Charlemagne had spent months planning the American participation in the Regatta and he was not disappointed. In addition to privately owned yachts, there were four battleships of the United States European Squadron—the *San Francisco*, the *Chicago*, the *Machias*, headed by Rear Admiral Cotton's flagship, *Kearsarge*. Their stark white hulls contrasted with the dark gray, and much more numerous, ships of the German fleet which included eight ironclads, eight cruisers and ten other war ships.

In one race, Charlemagne was a guest on the Kaiser's sailboat, *Meteor II*, with several other Americans, including Cornelius Vanderbilt. The Kaiser was delighted when everyone aboard helped trim the sails and the *Meteor* won the race. The American newspapers reported enthusiastically that Americans, including the American Ambassador Charlemagne Tower, had saved the race for the Kaiser.

When the Kaiser paid a call on the *Kearsarge,* he was given a royal tour that lasted over an hour. From the *New York Herald* of June 26:

> As all naval men know, a feature of the Kearsarge is her two great superposed [gun] turrets. In the center of the stern [turrets], the Kaiser passed some time. Such turrets do not exist in the German navy, in which there are double turrets, but the upper one is stationary.
>
> The Kaiser watched with much interest the delicate mechanism whereby the ponderous structure could be turned, stopped and backed at will, fractions of inches, if needed, by just a small switch. He also took a keen interest in America's latest range finders.[4]

---

4.   The gun turrets on the *Kearsarge* that interested the Kaiser needed some fine-tuning. On April 13, 1906 a fire broke out in one of the turrets during target practice, taking the lives of ten officers and men. Although the *Kearsarge* was not used in combat in World War I, on August 18, 1918 she rescued survivors of a sailing ship that had been sunk by a German submarine. [Information from the Naval Historical Center web site].

Charlemagne arrived in the United States on the ship *Kaiser Wilhelm II* on July 14. He was quoted in the July 15, 1903 *New York Sun* on the subject of the regatta:

> It was a magnificent and splendid reception and one I wish more Americans could have seen. They would have had their eyes opened by the good feeling shown toward this country by every one, from the Kaiser down to the lowest sailor...
>
> The Kaiser is a great man, and if he were to visit this country he would carry everything before him...he is enlightened, broad-minded, progressive and, above all, democratic...
>
> The Kaiser made a minute inspection of the *Kearsarge*. He did it with the enjoyment with which one horseman would look over another's fine thoroughbred, admiring all the points...

Charlemagne immediately wrote Secretary of State John Hay inquiring whether he should make the trip to Washington. Hay replied from his summer place at Newbury, New Hampshire on July 22: "There is no reason why you should go to Washington in this torrid season. Our relations with Germany are happily so comfortable that they do not now need discussing..."

In September, Dominie and Roderick returned to the Fay School, Dominie having been promised a mid-year place at St. Mark's school if he had a good fall term.

Geoffrey had improved in general health during the summer, but his limp had increased. He now used crutches, and had a tight support, called a gaiter, buttoned around his right leg at night. Nellie and Charlemagne decided that in order to continue his warm salt air treatment, Geoffrey would spend the winter in St. Augustine, Florida, where he would stay at the Valencia Hotel with Hester Candler.

Charlemagne, his annual leave at an end, left for Berlin in late October with Helen and Gertrude and their nurse. The presentation of the statue of Frederick the Great had been postponed until the fall of 1904, because the statue was not yet ready.

Nellie accompanied Hester and Geoffrey to Florida. She met with the doctor who would attend Geoffrey and hired a Mr. Perkins as a tutor. When she was completely satisfied with the arrangements, she left for Berlin, arriving in mid-November. It was a wrench for her to again leave her boys for so long, and especially hard to leave Geoffrey in poor health in Florida, and separated from his brothers in Massachusetts.

Without Hester Candler, who had been with the family since Geoffrey was a little boy of seven, Nellie would not have been able to leave her son during the crucial period of his recuperation. But Hester, a trusted friend rather than a servant, would watch over Geoffrey's health like a mother hen.

Hester wrote Nellie every week informing her of Geoffrey's progress. By late November, she noticed a marked improvement in his appearance and energy. The tutor, she reported, was a success, and she had made sure that any new acquaintance measured up to what she considered the Tower family's standards. She deemed the other guests at the hotel, "a very nice group and suitable for Geoffrey to meet."

She added that Geoffrey was perfectly at home on his crutches and scared her to death doing stunts on them. By December, he could walk along with her comfortably without getting tired.

At dinner in the hotel dining room, Geoffrey had become a raconteur, telling stories of his and his brothers' experiences at school in Switzerland. The other guests thought the stories hilarious, but Hester worried that he might be a nuisance to the other diners. She soon found that the handsome blonde boy on crutches with the good manners won all hearts.

Geoffrey reported in one of his weekly letters to his parents: "I am getting on fine with my crutches. I never even think that I am on them, and…I never get at all tired with longer walks than I ever took with you…"

Dominie and Roderick spent Christmas with their aunt, Grace Putnam, in Philadelphia. At Nellie's request, eleven-year-old Roderick had sent a neatly penned Christmas list to her which included five things he would like for Christmas: "a new writing case, a picture of you in a frame, a small (cheap) traveling clock, a big knife and a fancy pen holder."

In Berlin, Nellie and Charlemagne gave a dinner in honor of the Kaiser on Dec. 3, 1903. It was said to be the first time the Kaiser had set foot in the home of an American ambassador. He stayed until after midnight and thoroughly enjoyed himself.

Charlemagne found the Kaiser infinitely more approachable than Tsar Nicholas II. The Tsar, a likable but shy young man, was unfailingly polite to diplomats, but never lost his reserve. In contrast, the Kaiser was ebullient, audacious, impulsive and very willing to share his opinions with Charlemagne.

On February 8, 1904, war was declared between Russia and Japan. The Japanese had attacked the Russian fleet at Port Arthur, an all-weather port on the Pacific that the Russians had leased from the Chinese. In the attack, the Japanese torpedoed two Russian battleships, *Tsarevich, Retvizan* as well as *Pallada*, a cruiser.

On hearing the news, the Kaiser immediately summoned Charlemagne to the palace to discuss the war. The result of the meeting may have had an influence on the United States's position on the need to protect China's neutrality. The *New York Times* carried the following article on Feb. 14, 1904:

> Berlin—The newspapers here discuss the question [of] who took the initiative in proposing that Chinese neutrality be respected in the Russo-Japanese War.
>
> While reports from Washington say that Germany took the lead, the semi-official *Berlin Post* asserts that the initiative was taken simultaneously by the United States and Germany. How it was possible for two powers to take the initiative is not explained.
>
> The truth seems to be that Emperor William, in conversation with Ambassador Tower, suggested that it would be an excellent thing if China were to be made inviolate in the war. The United States Ambassador agreed with his Majesty, and the suggestion was wired to Washington, where it was at once adopted. Then United States Secretary of State Hay, with the knowledge of Baron Speck von Sternburg, the German Ambassador at Washington, sent his now celebrated note to the powers…

Berlin social life was in high gear. Countless invitations written on stiff cards, embellished with coats of arms or insignia, arrived at the American Embassy almost daily from the Court, from other embassies and from friends in the international community. It would have been impossible to accept more than a fraction of them.

Nellie was becoming a hostess *par excellence*. She found the spacious Pringheim Palace ideal for formal entertaining on a large scale. Encouraged by the warm reception both she and Charlemagne received at Court, as well as in Berlin's diplomatic community, Nellie entertained often and lavishly.

From January through March of 1904, the Towers hosted a series of luncheons and dinners at their elegant Berlin home, all meticulously recorded by Nellie in a special book of menus and lists of dinner guests: On Tuesday, January 12, dinner for 30; Wednesday, January 27, a ladies' luncheon for 28; Wednesday, February 3, dinner for 27 with Prince and Princess Henry as honored guests and their large entourage as well as American guests and the staff of the American embassy and their wives; Thursday, February 11, dinner for 30, including the Kaiser; Tuesday, February 24 luncheon for 24; Thursday, March 3, luncheon for 20 ladies, Friday, March 4 dinner for 36 and Thursday, March 24, dinner for 40.

The *Washington Herald* for Dec. 9, 1906 described a guest's arrival at the Tower residence:

> On arriving at the embassy, the carriage door is opened by a footman in livery, and one passes into the house between two lackeys who stand at attention. An usher directs the guests to a dressing room, where deft maids help remove their wraps. This accomplished, the [calling] cards are handed to one of the ushers and passed by him to a secretary, who makes note of name, address, and day at home.
>
> Then begins the ascent up the marble stairway, carpeted with red velvet, between the liveried lackeys, who are stationed here and there along its length. At the door of the drawing room the guests are presented by the secretary of the embassy to Mrs. Tower and the Ambassador. It is all quite simple, but everything is so perfectly arranged that there is nothing to criticize.

Town and Country magazine, in its December 17, 1904 issue, described a dinner at the American Embassy on February 11, attended by the Kaiser:

> His Majesty...arrived at seven o'clock, accompanied by General von Plessen...General Count von Moltke, and Count von Schmittof, and he was received at the entrance by the ambassador, surrounded by the staff of the embassy. Mrs. Tower awaited...at the head of the central staircase where a distinguished company of ladies and gentlemen...were already assembled. The Emperor proceeded immediately to join the guests...and spoke a few words of cordial greeting to each one personally.
>
> The table, which was laid for thirty guests, and sumptuously decorated with masses of orchids and roses, was set in the large dining-room, opening into the conservatory. His Majesty had Mrs. Tower on his right hand...
>
> The entire diplomatic corps in Berlin regard the Kaiser's presence at this dinner a compliment to the United States...

In the winter of 1904, Helen, seven-and-a-half and Gertrude, just six years old, had settled happily into life in Berlin. They liked their governess and enjoyed attending a small private school across the Konigsplatz from the Embassy residence; their teacher was a Fraulein Morris. Both girls took dancing lessons from a Frau von Schubert and Helen studied piano. They had two little dogs to which they were devoted. Although they missed their brothers, they had each other, and, of course, their parents.

It was not so easy for Nellie and Charlemagne to direct the lives of the three boys, and to be certain they were being well educated. In the winter of 1904, all the reports were good. Dominie, after a year at the Fay School, was attending St.

Mark's School and was getting along well. Roderick, at the Fay School, was his usual exuberant self. Especially welcome were the reports from Hester on Geoffrey's continuing recuperation in Florida. "Geoffrey continues well and full of life and spirits, more than I can manage sometimes. He is a dear boy but is…too adventuresome on his crutches, and I have to lecture him…as I fear he might have an accident…he says he has an overflow of spirits," Hester wrote.

By May, the Tower boys could hardly wait for summer to begin and to have the whole family together at Waterville. They had missed their parents during the long nine-month separation, made more difficult for all of them by having Geoffrey in Florida. Dominie wrote to his father on May 8: "You cannot imagine how I am looking forward to this summer and being with you again."

Nellie, Helen and Gertrude sailed to the United States in late May; Charlemagne would leave Germany for America after the Kiel Regatta in June.

The Ambassador was in the final stages of preparations for Kiel, planning for the numerous American dignitaries and friends of the Towers who planned to attend the regatta.

Charlemagne received a request from his friend Anthony J. Drexel on May 26, "to secure for me a good berth in Kiel Harbor…the *Margarita* draws 17 feet 6 inches and is 1797 tons." On June 5 Drexel wrote again, thanking Charlemagne for the good berth he had secured and alerting him that "the Fred Vanderbilts are going…don't be surprised if you hear from them…he has a new yacht the *Warrior* about 1200 tons."

Andrew Carnegie, who had become a regular correspondent, wrote to Charlemagne on June 15, 1904 to say that he would not be able to go to Germany the following fall as he had hoped because he had to be in New York for a board of director's meeting. "I do greatly wish to meet that original, the Emperor, but cannot get to Berlin this autumn."

The much-heralded unveiling of the statue of Frederick the Great in Washington, D.C. was due to take place on November 20, 1904. The bronze statue was an exact replica of one that stood in the palace at Potsdam.

The planning had begun for the presentation in early March when Charlemagne had received a letter from Baron von Sternburg, the German Ambassador to the United States, soliciting Charlemagne's ideas for the ceremony of unveiling, and expressing his hope that the Ambassador would participate in the ceremony.

Charlemagne would have liked nothing better than to have a key role in the proceedings, and to be asked to speak as well. After seven years of foreign posts, he would welcome the opportunity to be on center stage in his nation's capital. It was clear that the Kaiser expected him to participate; not to do so would be very embarrassing for Charlemagne and could be considered an affront to the Kaiser.

However, Charlemagne's participation in an official capacity had to be authorized by the State Department. On Sept. 9, Secretary of State John Hay wrote Charlemagne that "the President would be glad to have you present at the unveiling..."

Being present was not what Charlemagne had in mind. On September 12, Charlemagne wrote to President Roosevelt:

> Mr. President,
>   Mr. Hay has communicated to me, in a note dated at Newbury, the 9th instant, your wish that I should remain in America until after the unveiling of the Statue of Frederick the Great.
>   I beg leave to thank you, and I shall postpone my departure accordingly in order to have the honor of being present upon that occasion.
>   With the assurance of my highest respect,
>   Very Sincerely yours,
>   Charlemagne Tower

The ambassador still needed a formal request from the State Department to allow him to extend his summer leave and participate in the ceremony with full rank. Had he been able to meet with Secretary of State Hay in Washington, he was sure the matter would have been settled easily. But Hay, an ill man who spent a good deal of time away from Washington, was not available.

Charlemagne wrote Alvey Adee, Second Assistant Secretary of the State Department, whom he knew personally, to find out whether he was expected to attend the ceremony as an invited guest or in an official capacity. Adee wrote back on September 19:

> My understanding of the Secretary's letter, and of his conversation with me on the subject, was that the President would be glad to have you attend the unveiling with full rank; but, so far as pay is concerned, the Treasury Department has repeatedly held that the statute gives no discretion to order an officer to remain on departmental duty beyond his statutory leave...

Pay was not the issue; Charlemagne did not want his leave extended as a personal favor. He felt that his attendance at the ceremony as American Ambassador to Germany should be required, not granted as a favor.

On September 22, Charlemagne wrote Adee a letter of considerable pique:

If Mr. Hay were in Washington, I think the shortest way out of my muddle would be, to go down there tomorrow or the next day to talk over with him the subject of my leave. I have been waiting several days, with the hope that I might hear either from you again, or from him directly. But my time is growing short; for if I return to my post in the regular way, I must sail on Tuesday October 4th, which gives me little leeway to get ready. I am inclined to go back to my post, and, under the present circumstances, that is what I prefer to do. It is evidently considered in the department, that an extension of leave in my case is a personal favor, and, while I am appreciative, so I have said before, I beg to decline. If you can send me any word to guide me, will you not please telegraph me tomorrow morning…

   I should like to know in this way, whether to <u>continue arrangements for my departure, October 4th;</u> whether I ought to <u>go to Washington to consult you or Mr. Hay</u> or whether I ought to <u>remain for the unveiling at all events.</u> I feel confident that you understand my position, and that I may rely upon your friendship, now as always heretofore.

Four days later, on September 26, Adee wired Charlemagne in Philadelphia:

   I feel scarcely competent to advise. The President said to Mr. Hay that he would be glad to have you stay for the unveiling. In informing you of this the department, owing to statutory conditions, refrained from directing you to remain but under the circumstances the formal leave which was necessarily granted may hardly be construed as a personal indulgence. Mr. Hay will not be in Washington before October fourth.

Charlemagne decided to stay longer in the United States, but his pride was hurt. He and Nellie went to Waterville with Helen, Gertrude, Geoffrey and Hester. Dominie and Roderick had already returned to school.

Nellie and Charlemagne visited locally, and on one occasion traveled by train to Utica, fifteen miles away, to have dinner with friends, returning the next day. In fine weather, the chauffeur drove them on short excursions in "the machine," a Buickmobile. When fall rains had quieted the dust on the dirt roads, Charlemagne enjoyed driving his team of gray carriage horses.

Charlemagne was considerably relieved when he received a letter on War Department letterhead, dated October 17, 1904, from Major General G. L. Gillespie, assistant chief of staff:

   At the request of the Secretary of War, it gives me pleasure to extend to you, in his name, an invitation to attend the ceremony of the unveiling of the Statue of Frederick the Great which takes place at 2:30 p.m. November 19 at Washington Barracks…The President will make the principal address, and will be followed by the German Ambassador and the Secretary of War, respectively, whose remarks will be limited to ten minutes.

The Secretary of War wishes me to say, further, that it would be acceptable for you to close the ceremonies by a few remarks…

Grateful to have received this face-saving invitation, Charlemagne immediately wrote General Gillespie to accept.

The Towers dined at the White House the night before the unveiling. The ceremony the next day was a success; President Roosevelt noted in his opening remarks that the Kaiser's gift would bring closer bonds of amity between the two nations. The silken cord attached to the covering of the statue was released by Baroness von Sternburg, the wife of the German Ambassador to the United States. *The North American*, Philadelphia, November 20, 1904, reported: "Baron Sternburg presented a striking appearance in his sky blue uniform with silver trimmings, and high boots and wearing the Tartar cap of ermine…" The newspaper quoted Charlemagne's remarks:

Ambassador Tower's Tribute

After referring at length to the influence of Frederick the Great upon the civilization of Europe, and to the sterling qualities of the man and his great devotion to his people, Ambassador Tower said:

"The enlightened and broad-minded German Emperor has sent us the statue of this great statesman and reformer as a present to the nation. His act expresses his own personal feeling of friendship toward the American people, his appreciation of American greatness and of our purposes in the advancement of civilization throughout the world."

Charlemagne, having considerably extended his leave, left immediately for Berlin, with the little girls and their nurse, Bertha. Nellie stayed a few more weeks in order to visit Dominie and Roderick at their schools and then to see Geoffrey and Hester off for Florida.

Parting from their parents was hard on all the boys. Roderick, now twelve-years-old, wrote to his mother on Wednesday, November 30, a few days after saying goodbye to her at the Fay School. "That certainly was a sad moment last Sunday night when we had to part, wasn't it?…I didn't feel very sad after supper on Sunday because I was thinking that you were in just such and such a place. I expect you are now in Philadelphia with Geoffrey…"

Charlemagne wrote to Nellie from the embassy in Berlin on December 8,1904 addressed to her at Garlant's Hotel where she would rest for a few days before continuing the journey to Berlin.

> My dear Nennie,
>
> We are thinking of you constantly, the little girls and I, counting the days until a message shall come to say that you are safely on land again. All are well and all has been going well with us since our return. The children fell very easily into their old life again, almost as if they had not been away...Berlin is quiet; nothing is going on as yet, nor are many people to be seen...
>
> The day after my return I went to see...Bulow[5], by appointment, to the latter of whom I said in the course of conversation, which naturally turned upon the unveiling in Washington and the gratification of the Emperor at the way in which everything had passed off, that I should not venture to ask for a special audience, but that if the Emperor wished to see me at any time I should be happy to place myself at his service.
>
> The next morning I received an invitation to dinner at the Bulows' and <u>that same evening</u> in company with the Emperor to which, of course, I went. It was a mens' dinner, only about twelve people at table...
>
> The Emperor was exceedingly cordial, and immediately upon his arrival, after saying good evening to the hostess, he came directly to where I was standing and said: "I have no words to express to you my thanks for what you have done!" As the company was a small one the conversation was necessarily more general, so that I had no chance to talk with him apart; but when he took his leave he shook hands as he went out, and said: "Remember, I thank you!" I feel that the incident in Washington was worth all that we had to go through...

On December 15, 1904, Charlemagne wrote to President Theodore Roosevelt relating how pleased the Kaiser was with the dedication and the President's remarks which, the Kaiser said, showed "an extraordinary understanding of the character of Frederick, all the more remarkable in the case of a historical student who is not himself a German."

---

5.   The German Chancellor, Prince Bernhard von Bulow.

Nellie Tower in 1905.

The Towers leased the Pringheim Palace, at number 4 Koenigsplatz,
as their residence in Berlin, 1902–1908. It was situated
across a broad boulevard from the parliament building,
near the Tiergarten.

Grand staircase, Pringheim Palace, Berlin.

Drawing room, Pringheim Palace, Berlin

Nellie Tower's boudoir at the Pringheim Palace in Berlin.

Kaiser Wilhelm II and Charlemagne Tower
at the auto races.

Princess Victoria Louise, "Sissy,"
daughter of Kaiser Wilhelm, invited
Helen and Gertrude to play at the Bellevue
Palace in Berlin, spring 1906.

Crown Prince William of Germany,
who danced with Helen and Gertrude
at Nellie's last Flower Ball at the
American Embassy in Berlin, January 1908.

17

Berlin 1904–1906

In January 1905, Russia and Japan had been at war for a year and there seemed to be no end in sight. The Russians had recently surrendered Port Arthur to the Japanese. In the months that followed the initial attack, the Japanese won battles at the Yalu River, at Dalny and at Liaoyang, causing the Russians to withdraw to Mukden. The Japanese victories surprised the international community that had taken it for granted that Russia would win. But Russia was waging war on a far distant front, connected only by thousands of miles of railroad, a part of which was unfinished.

After a meeting with Kaiser Wilhelm on February 4, 1905, Charlemagne wrote to President Roosevelt, to report that the Kaiser had told him that he had been approached indirectly by England and France

> to make encroachments upon China with a view to taking advantage of the negotiations that are likely to occur at the close of the war between Russia and Japan to seize by mutual agreement, and to occupy permanently, certain portions of the Chinese Empire…
>
> The Emperor said to me, however, that he considers the immediate danger to have been averted…the note of Mr. Secretary Hay to the Powers, [on the importance of maintaining the territorial integrity of China] at which he expressed repeatedly, throughout the interview, his highest gratification.

On February 16, 1905, President Theodore Roosevelt replied by letter to Charlemagne:

> I am interested in the conversation you report with the Emperor. I cannot believe that England has any intention of taking part in the partition of China, but there certainly do seem to be suspicious indications as to the possible action of France. I think the Emperor rendered a service by what he did.

The last battle of the war, the Battle of Tsushima, took place at sea, when the Japanese destroyed a Russian fleet that had sailed from the Baltic. Robert R. Massie described the battle:

> At two o'clock in the afternoon on May 27, 1905, the Russian fleet, led by eight battleships steaming in columns, appeared in the Strait of Tsushima between Japan and Korea. Admiral Togo, the Japanese commander, ranged his ships seven thousand yards across the head of the Russian columns, bringing his guns to bear first on one Russian ship, then another.... Within forty-five minutes it was over...[1]

The stunning success of the battle shocked Europe and America. A country such as England, whose main defense was the Royal Navy, might not be as powerful as was once thought.

The Kaiser was jittery as well. He sent Charlemagne a hand-written letter on June 4, 1905, marked "Strictly Confidential," which was delivered to the ambassador as he was leaving the cathedral in Berlin where he had attended a service in connection with the Crown Prince's wedding. The Kaiser feared that when the news of the Russian naval defeat became known in St. Petersburg that riots would ensue which could endanger the life of the tsar. "I have written him a letter counseling him to open negotiations for Peace," the Kaiser wrote Charlemagne, "at the same time I drew his attention to the fact that America was the *only* nation which is regarded by the Japanese with highest respect, and that the head of the American People would consequently be the right person to appeal to, in the hopes that he will be able to bring the Japanese down to reasonable proposals..."

The Kaiser, a distant cousin of the Tsar's and a first cousin of the Empress Alexandra, had little respect for the Russian ruler. The Kaiser was forever meddling in Russian affairs and had encouraged Tsar Nicholas to be more aggressive in the east, which he thought would keep Nicholas occupied while he, the Kaiser, concentrated on western Europe. But the ferocity with which the Japanese struck the Russians truly alarmed the Kaiser. If the Tsar toppled, so might other crowned heads in a terrible domino effect.

Both Russia and Japan agreed that the peace negotiations should be held in the United States. President Roosevelt acted as mediator at Portsmouth, New Hampshire; the Peace Treaty was signed on September 5, 1905. President Theodore Roosevelt was awarded the Nobel Peace Prize for his efforts as mediator.

---

1. Massie, 89.

In the spring of 1905, Charlemagne was seriously considering retirement. On May 18, he wrote to his mentor, Senator Boise Penrose:

> I want to tell you confidentially…that I think I should like to return to Philadelphia permanently next year. I have been away a long time now, at some sacrifice to my interests at home, which begin to require my presence there. My post in Berlin is exceedingly agreeable to me and I am happy in it—I could not have one that would suit me better in the diplomatic. My only reason for giving up is that I do not want to stay away so long from America…

At age fifty-seven, Charlemagne was in his seventh year as a diplomat, or "diplomatist" as he referred to his profession, longer than most American ambassadors at the time. Relations between the United States and Germany were very good—so good that there was little need for diplomacy.

The routine tasks at the embassy did not challenge Charlemagne's considerable intellect. Rather than exercising diplomacy, he found himself maintaining the status quo, meeting and greeting Americans abroad, arranging ceremonies and presentations, and dealing with the stream of good wishes and tributes that flowed back and forth between Germany and the United States.

In January 1905, the University of Pennsylvania notified Charlemagne that it wished to confer the LL.D. degree on the Kaiser at the same time that it conferred that degree on President Roosevelt. Charlemagne's reply by cable: "The Emperor will accept Degree. You are expected to invite Sternburg [the German Ambassador to the United States] to accept for him…"

In March 1905, the Kaiser sent President Roosevelt a collector's edition of *Niebelungenlied,* the great medieval German epic on which Richard Wagner based the Ring operas. President Roosevelt wrote to Charlemagne on March 13, requesting that he "call in person on the Emperor and express to him my great appreciation of the beautiful edition of the Niebelungen-Lied [*sic*] which he has just sent me through Ambassador Sternburg. Say to His Majesty that I could not have received a gift I would have appreciated more…"

Press coverage of events at the American Embassy was constant, on both sides of the Atlantic. The Paris edition of the February 28, 1905 *New York Herald* described the Towers' costume ball :

> One of the most brilliant entertainments of recent years in Berlin society… Among the costumes of the men should be mentioned especially that of the German Crown Prince, who had put on the uniform worn by his regiment at the time of Frederick the Great—an antique military dress with wig and white

gaiters— that produced a most agreeable effect in the midst of the surround-ings to which it was so well suited. Accompanying His Imperial Highness were Prince Joachim Albrecht of Prussia and a group of other young officers who wore the same uniform...

The American press enjoyed speculating on the cost to the Towers of main-taining such an extravagant life style. The Atlanta, Georgia *Journal* ran an article on Dec. 15, 1905:

> Charlemagne Tower, in Berlin, is the first American ambassador to Germany to rival the magnificence of the British, Russian and Austrian embassies...he pays $18,500 a year rent, has 37 servants, all wearing gorgeous liveries with a tower for a crest on the buttons. One of Mr. Tower's servants always wears at his side a Turkish scimitar, his badge of office as superior butler...[he is] one of the sights of Berlin. Mr. Tower spends $100,000 a year on entertaining...[which includes] two balls a year attended by members of the royal family.

Dealing with Secretary of State John Hay, who had been ill and often absent from his post for the better part of the last two years, was a continuing frustration for Charlemagne. On May 12, Hay wrote to the ambassador from the German spa Baden Mannheim where he was taking a cure. Under normal circumstances the vacationing Secretary of State would have taken the opportunity to meet with German cabinet officials, strengthening the American position in Berlin, but Hay wrote to Charlemagne, "My doctor has just told me that while I am doing very well indeed I must not think of making any break in my cure, and must avoid any social or official engagements." He requested that the ambassador not men-tion his presence in Germany to the Chancellor, Count von Bulow, as he was too ill to represent the United States in an official capacity. Charlemagne went to Baden Mannheim to see Hay; it was the last time the two men met.

Nothing was settled about Charlemagne's retirement. The Towers decided to stay in Germany that summer to compensate for the long leave Charlemagne had taken the previous summer and fall.

In the spring of 1905, Charlemagne and Nellie prepared for the arrival in Ber-lin of Geoffrey and Hester for the summer. Geoffrey, who would be fifteen in July, had been attending the Adirondack-Florida School during its winter semes-ter in Coconut Grove, Florida. Although he could not participate in school sports, he could attend classes. For exercise, he was allowed to take long walks, fish and sail. According to his diary, he managed to augment his approved exer-cise program with activities that were strictly forbidden—roughhousing with the other boys and jousting with his friend Dex, by putting a boxing glove on the end of a crutch.

Dominie would have to stay in the United States in order to attend summer school. He had found St. Marks too difficult and in the fall would transfer to Exeter, considered by his parents to be an easier school.

Geoffrey and Hester arrived in Hamburg on May 1. Geoffrey was examined by two German specialists, Dr. Hoffer and Dr. Schhyler, who agreed that the boy no longer needed crutches. Charlemagne was not so optimistic. Geoffrey noted in his diary that "Father held to the fact that Dr. Willard and Dr. Bennett [in Philadelphia] said that I would not be able to walk until the autumn, and so he agreed to have Dr. Hoffer write to Dr. Willard, and we would depend on his answer."

Roderick would sail to Europe in June after his final school term at the Fay School and a week's visit with a school friend in Rochester, New York. He traveled with Mr. Beck, an old friend of Charlemagne's who worked in the Tower Estate office in Philadelphia. On May 4, Roderick wrote to his mother that he was so happy that Geoffrey "had arrived safe and well. I was very glad to know that because I was almost sure that he would have a very long, rough, and hard trip."

Nellie planned a summer of study for Geoffrey, who would be fifteen in July and would be entering Exeter Academy in the fall. He had a German tutor, Herr Trantow, and an English tutor, Mr. Watts. His days fell into a pattern of study, walks in the park, trips to museums and observing the embassy activities.

On June 2, 1905 Geoffrey described in his diary watching the procession of Crown Prince William's bride to be, the beautiful dark haired Duchess Cecilia of Mecklenburg-Schwerin as she made her official state entry into Berlin, three days prior to the wedding day:

> This is a day which will probably be famous in history, as the coming to Berlin of the first Crown Prince's bride. Mother and Father went to the French Embassy to see her pass Unter den Linden and the rest of us all went to the Chancery [the office of the American Embassy] from where we got a fine view. She rode in a golden carriage on the right of the Empress. The carriage was pulled by eight black stallions and made a very beautiful sight. There were postillions on some of the horses, with powdered hair and fine clothes. The streets were crowded, and even the roofs of some of the houses were crowded with people. The Crown Prince rode past with part of his regiment. There were many royal carriages. I do not expect that I would forget today if I lived for a long time.

Nellie and Charlemagne left for the Kiel Regatta on June 21; Geoffrey recorded in his diary the luggage required for a week: "Mother and Father had seven trunks between them and a hat box, and the chasseur had one little tiny hand bag."

On June 29, late in the evening, while Nellie and Charlemagne were still away, Roderick and Mr. Beck arrived. In celebration, Herr Trantow allowed the boys to speak English instead of German on their morning walks, Geoffrey noted in his diary, but that was only "until Mother comes to enforce the law." With a twelve-year old brother as companion, Geoffrey's summer would not be all study.

The ailing Secretary of State John Hay died on July 1, 1905 ending a distinguished career of public service which included major work on the Open Door policy in China and on the creation of the Panama Canal while serving as Secretary of State under presidents McKinley and T. R. Roosevelt.

At the end of July, 1905 Nellie and the children embarked on a five week sojourn in Germany, to Wernigerode, an old town in the foothills of the Harz Mountains, to Frankfurt, Heidelberg, then to Main and by boat to Cologne where they stayed at the Hotel du Nor.

Nellie was anxious to find a suitable boarding house where the little girls could stay with their governess when she accompanied the boys to America in September and Charlemagne would be in England. She chose the Charlottenheim in Berlin, which Geoffrey described as a "place…for old or very young people, but a little slow for us."

Nellie sailed for America in early September with Roderick and Geoffrey, where they were all reunited with Dominie. She helped her oldest son settle into his new school, Phillips Exeter Academy in Exeter, New Hampshire, and installed Geoffrey and Roderick at Middlesex, in Concord, Massachusetts.

In Berlin, Charlemagne was relieved to hear that President Roosevelt had appointed Elihu Root Secretary of State. Root, whose family lived in Hamilton, New York, only a few miles from Waterville, Charlemagne's summer home, knew Charlemagne personally as the two families had been friends for many years.

On September 27, Secretary of State Root wrote to Charlemagne:

> …I expect to begin my duties in Washington next week and to take up the Commercial Treaty [with Germany] very promptly. There has been a suggestion that a special commission should be sent over to enquire into the situation, but I think it ought to be done through you, and the President has assented to this. You will presently receive an official communication on the subject. The President is much interested in it and my personal interest in the

Ambassador from Waterville gives me a strong desire that the President shall be gratified by a prompt and thorough piece of work.

We feel very friendly to Germany of course, but they are very keen and aggressive competitors, and it is very important to know just how far they are bluffing, and so far as possible, just what cards they really hold.

Work on the treaty with its many complex questions of tariff reform would give Charlemagne a welcome focus, and easy communication with the State Department was a certainty with Root as Secretary of State. Charlemagne postponed any thoughts of retirement for the time being.

On October 17, 1905, Charlemagne went to Edinburgh to receive an honorary degree of Doctor of Laws at St. Andrews University. Andrew Carnegie had written to him on August 5 from Skibo Castle to give him details of the ceremony: "You are in goodly company. Bishop Potter is to receive a degree, and also the Archbishop of Canterbury."

There had been cheerful letters from all three boys that fall. In a December 3 letter from Dominie to his mother, he reported on Thanksgiving:

> One of the pleasantest…I have had for a long time [spent at the home of a family friend in Boston named Crosby], I might even say the pleasantest for a long, long time, because at last we three boys were together again even if we did not have you and Father.
>
> You wanted me to be sure to tell you all about Geoffrey and Roderick. Well, I think they have both much improved in more ways than one. Geoffrey still has that quiet, stock reserve which he has had in these last years. The moment I saw him I was impressed with his manly and handsome face…he looks well and seems happy, which is the main thing…
>
> Roderick is the little boy of old, laughing and joking and always playful. I must say that I could not find any fault in him—although I do not put myself up to be a critic— excepting that as usual he has a great hunger for olives. But I don't believe he ate more than a hundred.
>
> As we left them at the station and were coming home, Mr. Crosby said: "I like Geoffrey more every time I see him, for he is as honest as the day is long." and I said, "Yes, so do I."

Geoffrey wrote to his mother a week later:

> I have thought today of the happy Christmases that we have had in the past. I have thought of the ones on which we were not together, and I certainly do not think that we will have many more of that kind…it is nice to think that in this dear old city we will have plenty more happy family Christmases.

I really do love Philadelphia more than ever and like to think of the fine times we will have here when we are settled in our own home.

Roderick, who was thirteen, wrote a hurried note concerning matters of the heart: "There is a girl named Helen Perot who is perfectly beautiful and I simply <u>love</u> her. If I have ever (though I am pretty young) fallen in love or known what it is, it is now. I simply adore that girl."

Geoffrey wrote to Hester on December 17 at her home in Brooklyn, New York, giving her a report on school: "Last term I stood third in my class, and am my class editor of the 'Anvil,' I have a little collie…who knows me very well, and, I think loves me quite a little."

January of 1906 brought more good news from the boys. Dominie, who had developed a paternal attitude to his two younger brothers, particularly Geoffrey in his continuing recuperation, wrote to Nellie on January 14 from Exeter to report on a visit he had paid to Geoffrey and Roderick at Middlesex.

> My chief reason for going was to be sure that Geoffrey's brace was not hurting him or giving him any trouble at all. I also thought I might cheer them up by seeing them. But I was surprised to find how happy and contented they were. When I got there I found Roderick outside in a sweater, looking as healthy as could be…Geoffrey was down on the ice with his dog. I am sure he felt sorry at not being able to skate around with the other fellows, but as usual, he put on a bright face and tried to make the best of it. He assured me that his foot was all right and did not trouble him…

Mr. Peabody, a family friend who was a professor at Harvard, invited the three boys for Sunday lunch. He wrote Charlemagne on March 13 to tell him about the boys:

> Your oldest boy [Dominie] is quiet, controlled, straightforward, and unspoiled; and it was beautiful to see how much the others leaned on him, and how judicious he was in advising them. The second boy [Geoffrey], seems most like you in appearance and was gay and happy, but rapidly maturing into thoughtfulness and responsibility. His care of his little brother was that of a mother and no doubt, his invalidism has softened and ripened him. He seemed well, and paid little regard to his decreasing lameness. The little boy [Roderick] walked straight into our hearts, partly for his own sake, and partly because he is just the age and figure and coloring of our little boy taken from us seven years ago in Florence. They all seemed to fall into the family life easily, and prattled and chattered to our great delight. It was like beginning family life over again. And we felt all day how great a sacrifice you and Mrs.

Tower are making for the good of the country to separate yourselves so long from these growing and maturing boys.

In Berlin, the winter social season was in full swing. On January 20, 1906, the Towers gave a dinner for 44 guests, on the 28th a dinner for 38, and on February 21 they hosted the Flower Ball for hundreds of guests. On March 7 they gave a dinner for 64, on the 13th a dinner for 20. In April the Kaiser joined them for dinner on the 5th, later in the month they gave a dinner for 20, a lunch for 60 ladies, and dinner for 26 before departing for the Olympic Games in Athens, Greece. After the Olympics, they visited Istanbul where the Sultan of Turkey conferred on Nellie the Grand Cross of the Shefaket, which honored a woman's devotion to duty.

Nellie wrote to Geoffrey from Istanbul on May 3, thrilled with a good report she had received from Dr. Bennett; Geoffrey could give up his leg brace completely in September. She wrote:

> when you dress in the evening [the Tower boys wore tuxedoes when dining with their parents]…I know how happy you and I will be to see the end of the brace. I know you understand, do you not precious boy, from what Dr. Bennett has already told you that you must not expect to play football, baseball or tennis next winter? He will allow you, I believe, to ride horseback or skate and possibly a few other things which you can discuss with him…

In Constantinople, she wrote, dogs lived in the streets, pigeons were sacred and the Sultan, who had reigned for 30 years, had not left the palace except to go to the mosque. They would leave for Munich soon, she said, then go home to Berlin. "Then only six weeks before our darling boys arrive."

In the summer of 1906, the Tower family was together in Berlin. Even with a house full of children the business of the embassy continued to occupy Charlemagne. He was engrossed in his work on the Commercial Treaty, but summer meant Americans arriving to visit Europe. When they were prominent, or thought they were, they contacted Charlemagne in hopes of meeting the Kaiser.

One such was William Jennings Bryan, a leading member of the Democratic Party who in 1900 had run against McKinley and lost. He had to be firmly, but diplomatically, refused his request to meet with the Kaiser. Charlemagne wrote to Bryan, saying that the palace had informed him that the Kaiser would be involved in Cavalry maneuvers, but Charlemagne added a more candid explanation couched in diplomatic language:

If you were simply an American gentleman and not Mr. Bryan in addition, the matter could much more easily have been adjusted. But as you are today the most prominent and distinguished statesman of the Democratic Party, you are looked upon in Europe as the Leader of the Opposition, and the advisers of the Emperor could consider that an audience now would...[be seen as] interference upon their part in foreign...politics...Foreign Statesmen in active political life at home are never, or very rarely, received by the Sovereign in this country.[2]

Frequently an American ambassador from another embassy would alert Charlemagne of a prominent American about to arrive on his doorstep. J. Whitelaw Reid, the American Ambassador to the Court of St. James had a lengthy correspondence with Charlemagne in June, concerning the visit of Theodore Roosevelt's daughter Alice and her new husband, Nicholas Longworth, who would be visiting England, and Germany, but nobody knew quite when.

Such visits as these required embassy receptions for which Nellie arranged the appropriate tea or luncheon or dinner, with, and sometimes without, a suitable amount of notice.

With the fall came the painful parting from the boys. Nellie had planned in advance for their Thanksgiving and Christmas vacations, and later in the year, she would decide where they were to spend the spring vacation. She counted on the support of family and friends, and must have realized, as the boys grew older, that it was often difficult for the host family to provide enough diversion for the boys without completely upsetting their households. At times like these, Professor Peabody's words, "how great a sacrifice you...are making for the good of the country to separate yourselves so long from these growing and maturing boys" must have rung in her ears.

The boys were especially homesick when they first returned to school in the fall. Writing to his mother on October 7, 1906, Dominie expressed what he and his brothers were feeling:

Well, Sunday has come around again, the day on which I always write to you...I'll tell you it felt nice to hear from you and to know you all were thinking about us. It's funny, but sometimes you can't imagine how blue I get, thinking about the summer, and particularly on Sunday. I suppose because we always consider it your day.

---

2.   From a hand written copy of a letter from Charlemagne Tower to W. J. Bryan, June 9, 1906.

Dominie was again having trouble in school. Mr. Crosby had visited, Dominie wrote, and Mr. Watts as well, "who even offered to come up and help me."

Dominie suffered the most from the separation from his parents. His constant school problems were blamed on laziness and inattention although today he would probably be tested for dyslexia. He took his role as first-born very seriously. As the grandson and son of two other Charlemagnes whom he considered great men, he longed to live up to his parents' expectations, but as far as school was concerned, he did not know how to study. His happiest times were when he was with the whole family where he could receive the love and affection he craved and the acceptance that he needed.

The boys spent Christmas with Aunt Emmie and Uncle Tom Reilly in Philadelphia. Nellie wrote Geoffrey at the Reilly's on Dec. 20, with news of Hester's marriage to George Webb:

> They are to return to Balsham [in England] and to America in January. I never saw Hester look brighter…The new governess seems very sweet and capable and I am sure she will do well…I am very very busy preparing for Christmas—I believe we are to make 200 people happy on Christmas day— it is work but the joy of doing it is great.
>
> This is the shortest day of the year—after Jan. 1st, each hour brings us nearer to you my darling boys…Remember one dear son must write mother or father, or little sister each day so that I know all about your lovely visit [at the Reilly's]…the weather is very cold and very dark, but Christmas thoughts and occupations keep everyone busy and light hearted. I grieve only for my darling absent sons—Love to all,
>
> Your devoted Mother

In early April, Helen's little dog died suddenly. The girls were miserable until the Kaiser came to their rescue. The *New York Herald*, Paris edition, April 10, 1906 gave this account:

KAISER MAKES GIFT TO TWO LITTLE GIRLS

> A short time after the Emperor's arrival [for dinner at the American Embassy], while he was conversing with his host and hostess, the doors of the reception-room were suddenly flung wide open and a tall lackey, in the Imperial

livery, appeared on the threshold carrying a cushion on which there was a silk-lined basket containing one of the daintiest of terriers.[3]...The Emperor called the Ambassador's two little daughters to him and handed them the small animal, saying humorously: "Don't pull his ears too much or they are sure to fall off..."

The little girls were overjoyed and almost forgot all decorum in their profuse thanks to the kind donor. This thoughtful act of the Emperor was prompted by the knowledge, conveyed to him, that the children were almost broken-hearted by the recent death of a canine pet through poison.

The Kaiser, who loved children and had seven of his own, had developed a warm relationship with Helen and Gertrude. According to the *Washington Herald* of Dec. 9, 1906, "shortly after the Towers moved to Berlin and the Kaiser learned that the little girls were in residence he had sent in the royal coach and delivered to the door a box of toys for the girls for Christmas which he had selected. Since then, he has always remembered them at Christmas, and no subject in his empire is more loyal or devoted to him than these daughters of the American Ambassador."

In the spring of 1906, Helen, twelve and Gertrude, ten, were invited to Schloss Bellevue, one of the royal palaces in Berlin, to play with the Kaiser's only daughter, the fifteen-year-old Princess Victoria Louise, called Sissy by her family. Helen wrote to her mother who was vacationing with her father and Emma and Tom Reilly in Italy, Helen noted that "the Princess who is now fifteen, wears quite long dresses."

> Dear Momsy!
> It was lovely at the Schloss Bellevue...we went to see some lovely horses and afterwards the Emperor and the Empress came in an otomobile [*sic*] to the Schloss Bellevue and the Emperor asked me if my little dog snored in the night and I said no. The Emperor and the Empress got on horseback and they and some other officers went out riding.
> Afterwards we went and played something like Blind Mans Bluff...When we came home we had our two dear little dogs upstairs. My little dog is so happy, he played with Carlo...This afternoon we went to the Palace again. The Princess and we and some other girls made a little theater. Tomorrow

---

3.   The puppy described by the *New York Herald* was not a terrier but a brown dachshund, which the Tower girls named Flockie. He lived to an old age and fathered numerous litters of puppies. In July 1913, Albert Spengel, returning to Germany to visit his family, was entrusted by Charlemagne with two of Flockie's puppies as a gift to the Kaiser.

they are going to [give a play] for the whole royal family…The Princess's governess asked us if we could come and play with the Princess in the holidays. Goodbye Momsy!!!

From your loving daughter, Helen

18

Berlin 1906–1908

In January 1907, the news from America was discouraging: Dominie was still having trouble in school, and Geoffrey, at Middlesex, had received an unsatisfactory report. Nellie wrote to Geoffrey on January 24:

> My darling Geoffrey,
>
> I have written Mr. Taylor by this same mail and I hope I am right in assuring him that you intend to do better work this term.
>
> The fact that you conquered Algebra last autumn is such a good sign and shows that you can accomplish great things when you set about them with great determination. Now keep it up with everything and you are sure to get ahead…Stand up to your work in a manly way and conquer your difficulties.
>
> I am so glad to hear you have so much affection for dear Dominie—it may help to turn him in the right path just at this most critical moment. He has such a splendid nature and if he would only throw aside those habits of idleness and get to work he might even yet accomplish great things.
>
> Papa is so occupied over the tariff questions here and is having a good chance once again to add to his wonderful reputation as a diplomat and statesman.
>
> Helen and Gertrude are lovely these days, so happy and gay and the new governess is charming…
>
> Papa is quite well again but we have had such bitterly cold weather, he has not been allowed to walk out in the air—it was even too cold to go skating. Good night my dear, darling boy—love to Roderick.
> Your devoted Mother

In early February, Charlemagne met with the Kaiser to discuss The Hague Peace Conference that would take place in Holland later in the year. The major focus at the meeting would be disarmament, and the Kaiser was eager to have the ambassador explain to President Roosevelt why Germany strongly opposed disarmament.

After the meeting, Charlemagne reported to Secretary Root in a letter marked Private and Confidential. Instead of sending it in the official mail packet to the State Department, he mailed it first to the Tower offices in Philadelphia with instructions to forward it immediately to Mr. Root in Washington. The security measures give an indication of the importance of the information. The following quotations come from a pencil draft of Charlemagne's letter to the Secretary of State:

> There are certain things that largely influence the policy of Germany in its relations to the coming Hague [Peace] Conference…I venture to take this means of letting you know what I see and hear in Berlin, especially in regard to…disarmament and [Germany's] determination not to allow it even to be discussed at the Hague…

Charlemagne said the two influences which dictated Germany's foreign policy were the threat posed by Japan and Great Britain's foreign policy.

> The Kaiser feels that Japan could be a serious threat to Europe and…sees the extent of Japan's domination in Manchuria, and Siberia as well, where well-trained Japanese troops are swarming into Siberia under the guises of workman and servants…ready at a moment's notice to develop into a formidable armed body which the Russians have no means beyond the Urals to prevent them from falling entirely under the influence of Japan.
>
> A nearer and much more prolific source of anxiety to Germany lies in the political movements of the King of England…The British think that Germany is building her navy to fight them, and the Germans think that they shall never be safe until their ships are strong enough to protect their country against England.
>
> In the coming Hague Peace Conference, England plans to propose that each Power shall agree to maintain its present naval establishment and to build only a certain number of ships that may be allotted to it…To this the Germans reply: "The British Navy is already superior to ours, and if we agree to increase only in proportion with them we shall remain relatively where we are now. It is only a trick by which the English hope to keep ahead of us!"

On Thursday, March 7, 1907, the Emperor dined with the Towers, arriving according to the *Berliner Zeitung* of March 8, "with a bouquet and two photographs of himself in the costume of the time of Frederick the Great for his hostess and toys for the children."

Nellie and Charlemagne sailed for America the last week in March, for a stay that would last over a month. They would visit their boys at their respective schools and Charlemagne would meet with President Theodore Roosevelt and Secretary Root in Washington.

On April 8, 1907, Charlemagne was the guest of honor at a large dinner at the Manhattan Club in New York, given by Herman Ridder, publisher of the German-American newspaper, the *New-Yorker Staats-Zeitung;* on April 10th he attended a dinner hosted by Andrew Carnegie for leading foreign delegates to the Peace Congress.

For Charlemagne, the most important event of the spring visit was the weekend of Saturday, April 13, in Washington. That morning he met with Elihu Root and President Roosevelt. No doubt one of many topics discussed was Charlemagne's successfully completed work on the Commercial Treaty with Germany, which was made public a week later. After the meeting, Charlemagne and Nellie lunched at the White House.

After three days of luncheons, teas and dinners in their honor in Washington, the Towers left for Philadelphia in mid-April for another round of parties given by their old friends.

Charlemagne had two more speaking engagements to fulfill, both in Philadelphia. On April 20, he addressed the American Philosophical Society; on May 2 he spoke at the Wharton School of Finance and Economy on "Diplomacy and Diplomatic Usage."

Nellie fell ill during this period; on April 24, Dominie wrote to her from Exeter, urging her not to overdo after having such a close call. He was reassured when he saw her on Friday, May 10, when she and Charlemagne visited him at Exeter. Charlemagne, an alumnus of the school, gave a talk to the faculty and student body.

A few days earlier Charlemagne had paid high praise to the Kaiser in an interview with a *Washington Post* reporter, (quoted in the May 5, 1907 *Albany Press.*)

> ...The Kaiser is one of the greatest men of our time...The head of the German nation is thoroughly informed about everything that is going on, not only in Germany but throughout the world...he is as familiar with...the intricate problems of science, education, and sociology, as he is with those of statecraft...

Andrew Carnegie wrote Charlemagne from Pittsburgh on April 12 after he and the ambassador had met at the Carnegie dinner in New York:

> ...You told me you thought I should visit the Emperor. I leave that to your decision, asking you however to learn whether it would be agreeable. President

Roosevelt said to me he sometimes thought if he could only disregard precedent and get over there to talk with the Emperor and may be one or two others combined they could work wonders. I think he may yet decide to do it, genius and moral purpose united as in him should make precedents and I shall urge it upon him.

...I leave all this with you, feeling it will be my duty to go to Berlin if you so decide—

Instead of meeting in Berlin, Carnegie finally met the Kaiser at the Kiel Regatta in June. Carnegie and his wife and the Towers stayed at the Hotel Seebadeanstalt; the Carnegies joined the Towers in two dinners with the Kaiser—one on the royal yacht *Hohenzollern* and, at the Emperor's request, on a private yacht belonging to the Goelets.

In the course of the stay at Kiel, Carnegie felt that some misunderstanding had taken place between himself and the Kaiser; it probably had to do with Carnegie's fervent hope that Germany would work with England and the United States toward world peace, and agree to mutual disarmament.

On July 22, 1907, Carnegie wrote to Charlemagne, asking him to intercede with the Kaiser to try to clear up the misunderstanding. Carnegie felt strongly that Britain, the United States and Germany should be a trio working toward the same goals.

> I recognize what the Emperor has often proclaimed—Britain, Germany and America are of one race and should never forget that. Blood with me is very much thicker than water...would that Germany, Britain and America could be drawn close together—the two last are today closer than ever since the Revolution. Our aim should be to embrace the third in the circle. What could not the Emperor, President Roosevelt and Campbell Bannerman [the British Prime Minister] accomplish if they cooperated in the coming conference in the direction of Peace. Anything is possible if the Emperor joins with the two members of his race, that he is to play the great part in modern [times] has been my conviction for years...

In the summer of 1907, Charlemagne again considered retirement, and this time he would not put it off. He and Nellie had been apart from their sons for too long. The separation of nine months each year made it impossible to stay in close touch with the boys and they saw the bad school performances as symptoms of their sons' need for their family.

Charlemagne wrote to President Theodore Roosevelt on September 19, 1907 tendering his resignation effective the following spring, citing the needs of his family and his personal business affairs. In closing he said, "I should like to remain in Berlin during the coming winter...I think I shall ask your permission early in the summer to send my resignation to you."

President Theodore Roosevelt replied on October 9:

> ...I shall sincerely regret your leaving Berlin...I think you are absolutely right to go. I do not believe it is a good thing for a man to stay too long in the diplomatic service and away from his country, especially when he has growing children. You have given nearly twelve years' honorable service to your country. It is a fine record, and one of which you should be exceedingly proud when you hand it on as a memory to your children...

When announcement was made of Charlemagne's forthcoming retirement, the press was unstinting in its praise of his career. The *Public Ledger* in Philadelphia on Oct. 6, 1907, called Charlemagne "the best equipped, the most experienced and the most distinguished member of our present diplomatic service. His contemplated retirement will be a public loss..."

An editorial in the *Washington Post*, Thursday, October 10 said:

> The American Ambassador at Berlin, Charlemagne Tower, has represented this country with exceptional ability. Having won the confidence of the Emperor and of the foreign office, he has forestalled the trouble makers and sensation-mongers by frank explanations of American policies, and with military directness has asked and invariably received [clarification] on every move of the foreign office which he believed might prove susceptible of misunderstanding in Washington, and he has missed no opportunity to cultivate the good will of the German people. In a word, he has rendered precisely the sort of service for which an Ambassador is maintained.

The winter and spring of 1908 would be Nellie and Charlemagne's final months in Berlin.

The highlight of the American Embassy social season was once again the Towers' Flower Ball. The Crown Prince and Princess attended and danced all evening. Nellie wore a Gainsborough hat and a gown trimmed with garlands of purple and yellow orchids.

Nellie must have had a moment of melancholy as she surveyed the swirl of dancing couples at the last costume ball she would give in Berlin. She would miss the young people, especially. She herself never danced, but it had given her great pleasure to watch the slender young women in their elegant gowns and the German officers in their dress uniforms glide across the floor. She would miss having young American girls, the daughters of friends and acquaintances, stay at the Embassy during the Season.

That evening, Gladys Vanderbilt was one of the young Americans visiting the Embassy. During her three-week stay at the embassy, she would fall in love with the dashing Count Laszlo Szecheni of Hungary. [1]

Helen and Gertrude were allowed to make a brief appearance at the ball. Helen wrote to her brothers Geoffrey and Roderick at Middlesex on March 1 giving them a breathless description of the evening:

> …The ball was <u>beautiful!</u> We enjoyed it so much…First we watched the people come in, afterwards Mama took us in a little corner of the ball room where we could see the dancing perfectly. Suddenly, the Crown Prince came over and danced with Gertrude, of which I assure you I was not jealous as I would have been a year ago…[later] flowers were brought, then long sticks with roses for the ladies, then a little round ribbon with the colors—red, white and blue…it was when the flowers were given, that the Crown Prince came over and asked Mama which of us two he had danced with, for we looked so alike. Mama told him it was Gertrude so he gave me the flowers and danced with me. Papa put the bow of the flowers under his big dictionary for a week, then he put them in an envelope, and Mama will put them away amongst my treasures. We had a little crown of pink roses in our hair, and one around our shoulders. After the ball was over, we went up to bed, which was at two o'clock.

The *New York Herald* described the Tower girls in the February 23, 1908 edition: "The Misses Charlemagne Tower were in pink dresses trimmed with Japanese roses…to them the 'Prince *Charmant*,' as the crown Prince is known here, clicked his heels in the true style of a Prussian officer and invited one after the other to dance".

Dominie was in his final year at Exeter. Charlemagne assumed that his oldest son would go to Harvard as he himself and his father had. In fact, Charlemagne had already applied to Harvard's Randolph Hall for a room for his oldest son.

---

1.   In October 1908, Gladys Vanderbilt announced her engagement to the Count. She wrote Nellie before the public announcement: "My engagement…was so much due to your invitation to Berlin last winter that I want you to hear of it from <u>me</u>. We knew each other before but very slight, and had it not been for those three wonderful weeks in Germany this would probably never have happened…we are both very grateful to you."

But Dominie had other ideas. He wrote to his father on Feb. 12, 1908, presenting the case for going to Yale instead of Harvard. The letter is a model of respectful persuasion, and shows a good deal of self-confidence.

> Dad, I know you always wanted me to be frank and so I'm going to tell you exactly how I feel regarding the college question. About the only thing in Harvard I care anything about is the fact that it is near Boston...I don't like their spirit and I don't care anything about the crowd of fellows...I admire Yale for their democratic and fair spirit of play...I know a fine crowd of fellows there...from St. Mark's and Exeter...Of course around home Princeton is stronger than Yale or Harvard and there is no getting round the fact that it is a mighty fine college with a fine lot of fellows. Perhaps there being so many Philadelphia fellows here would slightly prejudice me in its favor...
>
> I feel that by going [somewhere other than Harvard] I could amount to more. For instance at Yale...they bring out a great deal more of what is in a fellow than at Harvard. They consider every side of a fellow, whilst at Harvard, as you know, they are greatly prejudiced as regards family, social position, the school you come from, etc. Now I am not saying that I should not have a good time at Cambridge and enjoy myself. No, on the contrary I'm afraid that is about all I would do...You are my Father and you shall decide.

On March 13, both the Kaiser and the Kaiserin dined at the Embassy, the Kaiserin for the first time, according a special honor for the Towers. The *Washington Post* noted on March 14, "the presence of the imperial couple was intended as a special personal compliment to the ambassador and his wife..." On the following Sunday, the Towers lunched with the Emperor and Empress at Schloss Berlin.

During the last week in March, newspapers in the United States and abroad were filled with the puzzling information that the German Emperor had rejected Charlemagne's replacement, Dr. David Jayne Hill, and named him *persona non grata*, having earlier said that Hill would be acceptable.

On March 26, *The New York Times*' banner headline read, "Germany Rejects Hill As Ambassador." There seemed no concrete reason for the rejection; certainly Dr. Hill had impressive credentials. He had once served as Assistant Secretary of State under John Hay, was an authority on international law, a former President of Rochester University, and had most recently been Minister to The Hague where he was responsible for compiling a history of world diplomacy.

It was hinted in the press that Charlemagne did not want to leave the post, that the Kaiser did not feel that the Hills had sufficient outside income to maintain the American Embassy, that Mrs. Hill was not acceptable; and it was rumored that Nellie did not want her husband to give up the post.

No one was more puzzled than Dr. Hill himself, who had been approved by the German Foreign Office.

By the end of March it had all been settled. On March 28, 1908 *The New York Times* reported, "BERLIN PREPARED TO WELCOME DR. HILL." The blame, the article stated, was laid at the feet of the Kaiser. The article concluded that the Emperor's concern that the Hills could not support the Embassy in the manner to which the Kaiser had become accustomed was a paramount reason.

Mrs. Hill, the article stated, was thought to be a poor choice: "Mrs. Hill was a giantess so far as learning and culture were concerned, but hopeless as a diplomatic hostess…One story which has provoked cynical smiles in Berlin society relates how Mrs. Hill's first appearance at the Hague consisted of a surprise visit early one morning when she appeared at the American Legation on a bicycle, clad in divided skirts, and announced herself as the wife of the new American Minister."

Charlemagne and Nellie probably were disappointed with the appointment of Dr. Hill as Charlemagne's successor. It was well known that Hill did not have a large private income which the Towers had found essential to maintaining the embassy in a position of preeminence, and Mrs. Hill's lack of decorum, an important quality in an ambassador's wife, would have shocked Nellie.

Nellie had taken her job as social leader of the American community in Berlin seriously, smoothing ruffled feathers at times and lending a helping hand at other times. She had entertained visiting Americans graciously at luncheons, teas and dinners. In her six years in Berlin, she had given receptions for a thousand, and balls for several hundred. She had arranged regular small dinners to enable Charlemagne to confer informally with guests, who were often high government officials or members of the Court. She was fluent in French and German and had mastered the complexities of Court etiquette in three major European capitals.

Nellie found in the Kaiser a friend and admirer. To the press he had several times praised her as the "Von Moltke of society," likening her social skills to the battle skills of the famous Prussian general, Helmuth von Moltke. This had amused and pleased her.

The thought that the American Embassy might slip from the pinnacle it had achieved under their guidance was distressing to both Nellie and Charlemagne, but nothing could be done. It was time to go home.

In early April, Nellie began the long and painful process of packing up the Pringheim Palace. It would be hard to leave Berlin where she had watched her daughters grow from small children to young girls who now accompanied her to museums, concerts and plays. Helen and Gertrude, too, loved the life in Berlin.

On April 2, 1908, Nellie wrote to Geoffrey at Middlesex School:

> I know how very much surprised you will be to hear we are making our arrangements to leave our house the end of this month. In May, we are going to take [Helen and Gertrude] to Switzerland and remain through the month there and in Northern Italy. In June Papa will come back here and give his letters to the Emperor.
>
> In July, we expect to [all be together] in England at the Olympic games and go to Skibo Castle and then to St. Jean de Luz for the month of August.
>
> We have also decided to sail for America early in October as Papa wishes to be in Philadelphia for the elections—think of Helen and Gertrude going back and forth to Miss Irwin's School!...I am feeling sad at leaving Berlin and yet very happy to be coming "home." I'm sorry you will never see this charming house again!...
>
> Much love, your devoted Mother

Easter Sunday was on April 19; Kaiser Wilhelm sent a large Easter egg of flowers to the Embassy to mark the day. Nellie and Charlemagne left the next day for Dresden. On April 22, Nellie wrote to Geoffrey from the Hotel Bellevue Dresden in Dresden:

> The dismantling of the house in Berlin began this morning, so now when we return we shall find the changes here already begun and our only wish will be to have the time go quickly until we leave with the children [for Switzerland] on Thursday, April 30th...Helen and Gertrude are often sad about our going but they will soon forget in the pleasure and interest of the new life in Philadelphia.
>
> I do not want to see my boudoir taken to pieces...how I love that room and I often wonder where next all those pretty things will be gathered about me. Many changes may take place in the next year or two.
>
> We are all so happy about next summer and if each one tries I should think we might have a great deal of real joy—to think of having Papa with us from beginning to end!
>
> Noise and bustle are going on all the time in the house now with many workers and busy servants. Good night darling boy—I certainly hope our next home will be as lovely as this one.
>
> Your devoted Mother

On June 1, 1908, Charlemagne was honored at a dinner at the American Association of Commerce and Trade. He spoke of "the community of interest which unites us all in the same purpose toward which we have striven together...the friendship, good understanding and cordial relations between the United States of America and the German Empire..."

On Saturday, June 6, Charlemagne made his farewell call on the Imperial Chancellor, Prince von Bulow. The following evening Foreign Secretary von Schoen gave an official dinner for the Towers at the Foreign Office.

On June 7, 1908, Nellie wrote to Geoffrey:

> Dearest Geoffrey,
>   This will be the last letter I shall ever write you on embassy paper—on Thursday next, the 11th; we shall leave Berlin for Paris.
>   Tomorrow your father and I are going to Potsdam to take luncheon with the Emperor and Empress and Papa will then hand in his letters of recall. This gives us a certain feeling of sadness, but we have no possible regret of any kind for we know we are doing what is right.
>   Now we shall be glad when all is over and we are established in Paris, for that is the first step toward our new life in America. It is eleven years almost to the day since we entered the diplomatic service!...Think of having Papa with us <u>all</u> the time...

On Monday, June 8, Charlemagne presented the Emperor with his official letters of recall. The Towers had traveled from Berlin to Potsdam on a special train, accompanied by the German Foreign Minister, von Schoen. *The New York Times,* in its June 9, 1908 edition, quoted the Emperor's remarks to Charlemagne: "I thank you for the exceedingly able manner in which you have managed the affairs between our countries for the last [six] years, as well as for the very great service that you have rendered in strengthening the friendship between us, and the brilliant way in which you and Mrs. Tower have maintained the Embassy in Berlin." After the formal ceremony, the Towers lunched with the Emperor and Empress and other members of the Imperial Family.

On Thursday, June 11, the Towers officially left Berlin for Paris. The June 12 edition of *The New York Times* reported:

> The station platform was filled with representatives of the Government and nearly the entire Diplomatic Corps in Berlin, as well as a large gathering of the American residents of the city...Foreign Secretary von Schoen presented Mrs. Tower with a handsome bouquet...Their compartment on the train was by then half filled with flowers.

Mr. Tower narrowly escaped being left behind. The train pulled out while he was standing to one side talking with friends, and he had to run and jump on board while it was gathering speed...

In the same article, the *Times* assessed Charlemagne's eleven-year diplomatic career:

Mr. Tower will be a hard man for any one to succeed. Socially he has set a pace which it will be difficult to equal and almost impossible to exceed, while he has contrived to win the personal good will of the Kaiser to a degree which has made him the most popular diplomat at the German Imperial Court...Few men in the history of American diplomacy have been able to look back upon more varied and valuable careers than Mr. Tower's.

19

Coming Home 1908–1910

Nellie and Charlemagne arrived at the Hotel du Rhin in the Place Vendome in Paris on June 19, 1908, with their daughters, Helen and Gertrude, the governess, Nellie's maid, and Charlemagne's valet. Crest, the chauffeur, would arrive a few days later with the automobile. Roderick, flushed with pride at having crossed the ocean alone, was the first to arrive from America, followed a week later by Geoffrey and Dominie.

The family first visited Andrew Carnegie at Skibo Castle in Scotland for four days, then stayed in London for a week to attend the Summer Olympics.

For the rest of the summer of 1908, the family traveled by automobile and train around England, France and Switzerland, in various combinations of family members. When they took the train, the chauffeur drove on ahead and met them at their destination. At one point Charlemagne's sister, Emma Reilly, and her daughter Joy motored with them in their own automobile.

To the three boys' delight, they were allowed to take excursions on their own, and stayed at the hotel in Paris for several days at a time with no parental supervision. Geoffrey told Hester Webb in a letter written at the end of August: "We have had <u>such</u> a nice summer, and it has been a pleasure ever since we left school. Now we have to go back to work, to say nothing of not knowing when we will come to Europe again."

Despite his poor performance at Exeter, Dominie would be entering Yale on his return, thanks to his father. In July, Charlemagne received a letter from the president of Yale, Allen Hadley: "We are delighted with the prospect of seeing your son here, both for his own sake and incidentally because of the frequency with which we hope it will bring you and Mrs. Tower to New Haven." Dominie had gotten his wish.

After the Tower boys returned to the United States, Nellie and Charlemagne and the girls stayed on in Paris until October, visiting friends and savoring the beauty of the city in fall.

When they arrived in the United States on October 19, 1908, Charlemagne faced eager reporters whose first question concerned his replacement, Dr. David Jayne Hill. Charlemagne had his statement ready: "Ambassador Hill is very popular and was well received by the Emperor...It is not true that a man has to be a millionaire to be an Ambassador," he told *The New York Times* on October 19.

The Towers stayed at the Hotel Bellevue Stratford while they looked for a suitable house. The girls attended Miss Agnes Irwin's School in Philadelphia.

Philadelphia Ledger society columnist Peggy Shippen noted the Towers' return in her column for October 25, 1908:

> It is refreshing to see a man after 11 years experience of the most exalted position among the foremost governing figures in the great political world—of which he was one—returning home with that simple gladness that home welcome gives the normal human being...one cannot help doing homage to the self-contained ex-Ambassador who returns home simply and quite guiltless of pose, after the most successful and brilliant of foreign careers, to claim his old place as one of us...

In May, the Towers leased a four-story brick and brownstone house at 1313 and 1315 Locust Street in Philadelphia.

Nellie's first task was planning the family's re-entry into Philadelphia society. As prominent members of the international community it would be a good deal easier than it had been twenty-one years earlier, in 1888, when Nellie Smith Tower arrived in Philadelphia as a new bride from Oakland, California.

In the intervening years, she had become an accomplished hostess who could converse in French or German as well as English, who could arrange an embassy reception for a thousand guests as easily as a small dinner for close friends.

From long practice, she was expert at turning a new house into a beautifully furnished home for family and guests. Although the house in Philadelphia was a good deal smaller than the embassies that had been her home for eleven years, it was considered large for a private home and Nellie furnished it with formal elegance.

Her first task was introducing her daughters to family friends. When she and Charlemagne left Philadelphia to live in Vienna in 1897, little Helen was three, and Gertrude was a baby not quite a year old. Unlike the boys, who had spent many school vacations in Philadelphia over the last six years, the girls were newcomers.

As soon as the move to the Locust Street house was complete in early December, Nellie arranged a formal tea to introduce fourteen-year-old Helen and twelve-year-old Gertrude to the family's old friends and their children.

All of the children would be included in Nellie's Young Peoples' New Year Party at the Hotel Bellevue Stratford on January 1, 1909. Nellie wrote on an invitation which she saved in a scrapbook, "This party was given to the five dear children upon our return to America after nearly twelve years' absence. 200 young people present."

Festivities were not limited to the children. Nellie's next project was a dinner-dance for adults at the Bellevue Stratford in late February for one hundred guests, followed, in mid-March, by a Sunday afternoon reception for several hundred friends at the house on Locust Street. In April, the girls served on a young people's committee that arranged a fair to benefit less fortunate children.

A personal glimpse into Nellie's style was given by Annette Wood Wright who as a young girl was a friend of the Tower girls. In a letter to a Tower cousin[1] she recalled her experience dining at the Towers':

> I remember being taken by my sister Letitia to have lunch with Mr. and Mrs. Tower at their house in Philadelphia. This was an interesting and enjoyable, if somewhat awesome, experience for little girls. I was told by Letitia not to ask for anything at the table, because there would be a footman behind every chair, who would watch to see what one needed…It was a large table, beautifully set with crystal and silver and very handsome china, and the meal was delicious and served in a style that surpassed my wildest imagination. I felt as if I were living in a fairy tale!
>
> The Towers often drove out of town on Sunday afternoons to visit my mother. She would serve tea in the parlor…one glorious day they brought me the most beautiful toy horse I had ever seen…covered with real horsehair.
>
> Mrs. Tower was a lovely and rather imposing lady, who wore large and beautiful hats, sometimes with ostrich plumes, upon which I gazed with admiration. They came and left in a chauffeur-driven limousine of the largest and most luxurious sort. I could not have been more impressed if we had had a visit from a real king and queen!

In addition to his personal business interests, Charlemagne was again in demand as a speaker, on subjects that included the American Revolution, international law and the diplomatic service.

---

1.   Mrs. Wright's letter Alfred Putnam on April 3, 1973.

In both lectures and newspaper interviews, he strongly advocated higher salaries for diplomats. An ambassador's salary should certainly be more than $17,000 per year, he argued. Although that sum was enough to live on, it was not nearly enough to entertain properly. Countries such as France, Germany and England paid their ambassadors three times as much and owned their own embassies in the major foreign cities. The situation would be hard to change, Charlemagne told the *Public Ledger* on November 1, 1908: "The American people are not much interested in foreign affairs or foreign relations. Their minds are set on home affairs, and they cannot easily be brought to see the importance of things that are so far away from home."

Among Charlemagne's many correspondents was his old friend Andrew Carnegie who wrote in reply to a letter from Charlemagne asking whether Carnegie's library project would extend to libraries in private institutions. Carnegie replied: "My library work is confined to Public Libraries strictly and if you came and saw the work that involves you would understand why I dare not extend the field. No sir, only libraries maintained by the people for the people..."[2]

In a letter written on November 14, 1900, Carnegie offered the former ambassador a new and interesting focus for his retirement years. He invited Charlemagne to become a member of the Board of Trustees of his newly created Endowment for International Peace, which would administer a trust of ten million dollars donated by Carnegie. The trustees would determine the distribution of the proceeds of the trust in the cause of world peace. Charlemagne accepted immediately and joined a board of twenty-eight leaders in business and public life, including President Taft. Elihu Root, also a member, would later be named president of the Endowment.

In May, Nellie and Charlemagne moved to the Tower Homestead in Waterville, New York, with Helen and Gertrude. The boys would join them there as they finished their school terms. The old family home in its beautiful setting of stately trees and formal gardens would give the family welcome relief from the heat of summer in Philadelphia.

Although entertaining was simpler in Waterville, Nellie still managed a full staff of household servants which included a cook, maids, butler, footmen, and laundress. The household servants lived in an eight-bedroom cottage behind the house. There was a separate cottage for the gardener and behind the carriage

---

2.   Andrew Carnegie, who had little formal schooling in his native Scotland, set up a $65 million endowment to build and fill 2,811 free libraries in the United States and other English-speaking countries.

house there were three single rooms for extra farm workers and a three-bedroom farmhouse.

The Homestead itself, which had only four bedrooms, was too small for the Tower family, now that they would be using it as their summer home. An architect was hired to design an addition that would add additional bedrooms and bathrooms and an informal living room.

Waterville, a town of just over one thousand inhabitants, was a peaceful place that offered little diversion except horseback riding and long walks. Charlemagne worked at his desk every morning. He was working a new book, a collection of essays. Nellie walked every day, sometimes for several miles, accompanied by whatever children and houseguests were at hand. She walked at a brisk pace, not a stroll.

Charlemagne's sister, Grace, and her husband, Earl Putnam, owned a summer home a few miles away; their children provided companions for the Tower children.

The Towers exchanged visits with friends in Cazenovia, Clinton, Hamilton and Utica, by automobile, with Crest at the wheel. In August, they rented a house in Islesboro, Maine for the month.

In the fall, it was a relief for Nellie and Charlemagne not to have to say goodbye to their sons for nine months. They looked forward to visiting them at their respective schools and taking a more active role in their lives.

With the eternal optimism of caring parents, they expected better school performance from the boys now that they were a family once again. But this was not to be. As the fall progressed it became clear that Dominie and Geoffrey maintained the same lack of interest in their studies as before, but now that their parents were closer geographically, they could no longer conceal it as easily. They both had private tutors to help them with their studies, but there was little improvement. Even Roderick, normally an able student, had a poor report.

Nellie was exasperated. She wrote to Geoffrey at Middlesex on October 29, 1909:

> I have not very good news from any of you boys. Mr. Fox wrote that you are a nice fellow and he likes you but you have only a very superficial knowledge of few subjects…you must take hold and work with spirit, earnestness and thoroughness! Listen to my warning in time!…
>
> Imagine if you had to tutor all summer or had to enter College with heavy conditions! <u>Imagine</u> this! Dominie cannot join any fraternity, as he is <u>not</u> a real sophomore—how this pains me. At present, we are having great trouble with his accounts—he wants money—always more and more— and refuses to

give an account of what he spends or requires. In the meantime we are getting enormous bills from Mr. Fox to be paid for tutoring extra hours and we sometimes feel—what is all this leading to?

Roderick's first report from Exeter is very unsatisfactory, most disappointing and I had to write him a letter yesterday of sharp reproof and warning. Do you wonder that I am not very proud or even contented for you boys seem to have no realization of your perilous attitudes?

Somewhat placated by Geoffrey's assurances that he would do better, she wrote to him again on December 3: "The house is lovely...It seems more beautiful to us each day and so I know how it must be to you also and I am sure we shall have a lovely holiday with you all."

Nellie wrote that she had planned a dinner party for him on Dec. 27, and listed the girls she had invited: "Bessie Wright, Marianna Lippincott and Gertrude Henry..." Before she had a chance to finish the letter, the afternoon mail brought more upsetting news. She continued her letter to Geoffrey:

A letter has come in from Mr. Gallagher, which has made us so unhappy and troubled about you. To be sure, it was written in your holidays at Thanksgiving time and so perhaps by now you are doing better as he seems to think you have promised to do.

Oh! Geoffrey—Do take life seriously and do your work to some purpose in life. You gave us no indication at Thanksgiving how very bad your lessons and marks were...Do be a man and at least be a creditable senior and leave your last year with some favor. No master wants a stupid, disobedient boy; everyone wants one who helps the credit of the school.

Roderick wrote what he hoped would be taken as a light and humorous letter to his father on December 5, requesting more money for expenses. "Dear Father, It is so long since I have felt money that I don't know what its soft and velvety surface feels like..." He gave an accounting of expenses—laundry bill, drug store, stationery and football shoes which added up to $24.25; he was taking a Wellesley College girl to the school dance and would need at least $5.00 for that.

Nellie and Charlemagne were clearly perplexed by the behavior of their three sons. As parents, they were new to the frustration of trying to please their almost grown-up sons on a year 'round basis.

The two older boys were rapidly becoming young men. Dominie, twenty-one, at Yale, was irresponsible about both his studies and his spending money.

Geoffrey, who five years earlier had been seriously ill, thin and pale, was now, at nineteen, strong and handsome. A slight limp was the only reminder of past illness. Having lost several years of school because of his illness, he was a senior at Middlesex. He, too, had become very independent and found it hard to fit in with his parents' plans.

After the spring vacation of 1910, Nellie, irritated that she had not heard from Geoffrey, wrote to him on Sunday, April 10:

> I am very much displeased because it is one week today since you left us and we have not had <u>one</u> line from you. We take it for granted that you reached school safely, that you are quite well, and that you thank us for your Easter vacation and that occasionally you think of those at home. We cannot sympathize with nor understand your apparent neglect and indifference.

Her unaccustomed tone of sarcasm reflected her hurt at what she considered his neglect of his family. She finally received a letter from Geoffrey thanking her for all she had done for him over spring vacation. Somewhat mollified, she wrote to him on April 17:

> I read between the lines that somehow your visit home this time did not give you all the pleasure you had hoped for. And you were not happy about the idea of the summer…but I trust upon reflection you realize that after all your father and I are trying to produce the best results with the materials at hand!

The "materials at hand" referred to the choices available for the family for summer quarters. The addition was underway on the house in Waterville and it would be uninhabitable until fall. Nellie thought that Northeast Harbor, Maine, would be a good choice for the whole family.

> It is not absolutely settled but we are negotiating for a house on the water's edge. Mrs. Pepper is not likely to trouble you with "social hindrances" as you like to call it, as they do not even arrive until the middle of July. Other friends tell us they have a riding master and several excellent saddle horses to hire and that the young people, principally girls, go out five or six at a time to ride—this will be very nice for Helen. There is also basketball, a squash court and a small baseball field.

On April 24, 1910, Nellie again wrote to Geoffrey on the subject of the summer plans:

> In a letter just received from Dominie, he expresses himself as rather independent about staying in Northeast. This pains me and I have written him

tonight that I consider it is the duty of each one of you to do all you can to make your father's summer a happy one.

Let us all take it for granted that it is going to be a success and look forward to it with proper zeal and pleasure. I am not trying to hurt you or Dominie but to make you happy—do give your father and myself the comfort we deserve to have. We are trying as hard as we know how to adjust our lives to the wishes and desires of our children—do support our effort and let us feel you are anticipating your family life this summer.

We cannot tell what may happen to make us sad—so let us rejoice and think if we are all spared to be together that that is the most important of all.

Spending the summer on an island on the coast of Maine with other young people whom their parents deemed socially acceptable held no appeal for either Dominie or Geoffrey, especially in contrast to the independence granted them on the European tour two summers before.

Geoffrey would have liked nothing better than to stay in Waterville for the summer. Having been denied school sports during his illness and recovery, he had since become an avid horseman and an excellent rider. He was completely happy in Waterville exercising the horses and doing as he pleased.

Geoffrey graduated from Middlesex with his class in June 1910. He would enter Yale in the fall. Charlemagne, Nellie and their daughters went to Concord, Massachusetts, for the graduation, then on to Maine.

The house in Northeast Harbor was indeed right on the water; friends with boats could anchor at the private dock. On July 22, the Towers gave a seated dinner for President and Mrs. Taft, who arrived on their yacht, "The Mayflower."

In September, Nellie faced the painful task of enrolling her daughters at St. Timothy's school in Catonsville, Maryland. It would be the first time she had lived apart from them. "It often makes me so sad to think next winter of this lovely home and not a child about me until the holidays," she wrote to Geoffrey at Yale.

Nellie and Charlemagne went back in Waterville for the fall. Nellie's sister, Ada, arrived from California on October 8 for a visit of several weeks.

The new wing on the Homestead added three bedrooms and a bathroom to the second floor and a guest bedroom and bathroom to the first floor, as well as another living room with fireplace. The house had also been equipped with central heating, which would make it possible to stay later into the fall. From the front, the new west wing was identical to the older east wing, with a matching facade in the Greek Revival style.

Charlemagne was still much in the public eye, especially since he had become a member of Carnegie's Peace Endowment Board. In February 1911, the Towers were guests of President and Mrs. Taft at a White House reception.

On March 9, 1911, Nellie received a letter from Helen Hadley, the wife of the President of Yale, who had invited Dominie and Geoffrey for dinner. She thought they were charming young men and interesting conversationalists. "You must be awfully proud of them; they talked politics at home and abroad, and literature, and poetry, and life in general, and were perfectly charming," she wrote. Reading the letter, Nellie must have enjoyed a moment of maternal pride.

Roderick was working hard in his last year at Exeter. He wanted desperately to go to Harvard. In September 1911, came the good news that he had been accepted at his father's alma mater for the fall of 1912.

The Tower Homestead in Waterville, New York after the west wing (left in the picture) was added in 1910.

The Charlemagne Tower family at the Homestead in 1912.
Helen sits on top step; Gertrude is with dog on bottom step. Geoffrey
is standing beside his mother. Roderick is in front of Gertrude;
Dominie is between Gertrude and Geoffrey.

20

Philadelphia 1910–1914
Family Scandal

Charlemagne had many good friends in Germany with whom he had kept in touch since leaving Berlin. Now that he served as a trustee of the Carnegie Endowment for International Peace, his ties in Germany took on a new significance.

On November 3, 1911, a telegram arrived at Waterville from Count Tiele Winckler inviting Charlemagne to a shooting party at Moschen, the Count's Castle near Kujan in Schlesia, Germany. The shooting party would take place from November 21 to November 25; Kaiser Wilhelm would be joining the party for part of that time. Count Winckler wrote, "Can you come and join the party—you have just time to catch the next steamer…"

Charlemagne wanted very much to go. He spoke in his diary of how flattered he was by the invitation "…the idea of seeing the Emperor again after an interval of nearly three years and a half…I said to myself that this opportunity was one that rarely comes to any one in a lifetime and might never come to me again."

Charlemagne decided to go, and to take Nellie with him. This may seem surprising since the invitation was to a shooting party. But under the terms of the Carnegie Endowment, trustees were encouraged to travel wherever they saw fit in the interests of peace, and to take members of their families with them, at the expense of the Endowment. By traveling as a couple Charlemagne may have hoped to give the trip a purely social perspective. However, the *New York Times* thought otherwise. On Sunday, November 26, 1911, the *Times* ran a front-page article: "TOWER ON SECRET MISSION? It is rumored that Mr. Tower is entrusted with a secret mission from President Taft to the Emperor, who regards Mr. Tower as one of his best American friends…"

After Nellie made a brief visit to Maryland to see the girls at St. Timothy's School, she and Charlemagne sailed for Bremen on the liner *Kronprinsessin*

Cecille, accompanied by three servants, one of whom was Albert Spengel, a German who had served in the embassy in Berlin and had gone with them to America.

The Towers first stayed in Dresden where they revisited places of interest. Charlemagne and Albert went to shooting parks in the countryside to test the guns Charlemagne would use. Nellie went on to Berlin when the two men left by train for Ober-Grogan where they were met by auto and taken to the Castle.

A foot of snow covered the ground on the first day of shooting, but peasants cleared the paths while the hunting party breakfasted. Charlemagne noted in his diary:

> Breakfast was partly in the English mode of cold meats on the table—ham, joints of beef, shoulders of mutton etc. and…also a great variety of egg dishes, chops, etc. which one takes, or not, according to choice…
>
> The Kaiser arrived by train in the late afternoon…A station had been created at the end of the main avenue of the park, where the railroad passes, about 3/4 of a mile from the castle door, for the Emperor to alight, which was decorated with festoons and colors, and there were arches across the avenue in the approach to the entrance to the castle door. A cordon of troops from a regiment stationed nearby formed lines to completely enclose the park; sentries guarded every road during the entire stay of the Emperor.

On November 27, Charlemagne wrote to Nellie who had gone on to Berlin, giving her details of his meeting with the Kaiser:

> The Emperor…looks exceedingly well and has changed very little…His greeting to me was just as cordial and friendly as in old times—When he saw me standing in the midst of the others, he opened his eyes very wide as he used to do, with feigned astonishment, and said: "How is this, America in Schlesia! How is Mrs. Tower and how are the children?…Tell Mrs. Tower that we still miss her very much in Berlin." He was most happy, too, when I told him that Helen and Gertrude had sent him their love. He even asked whether Flockie [the little dachshund the Kaiser had given the girls] is still alive and well.

Schloss Moschen, Count Winckler's castle near Kujan in Schlesia
where Charlemagne Tower stayed when he returned to Germany to
attend a shooting party with the Kaiser in 1911.

Charlemagne had several opportunities to converse with the Kaiser; on the evening of the Emperor's arrival, they had a long conversation alone late in the evening. The next day, the first day of shooting, Charlemagne sat next to the Emperor at breakfast.

Nellie had received an invitation from the Empress to go to the castle in Potsdam for lunch on Thursday. Charlemagne remained at Moschen for several more days before joining her in Berlin and returning to the United States.

It is not known whether the trip was for pleasure or if Charlemagne was, in fact, on a secret mission for President Taft. It is more likely that he wanted to go and was encouraged to go by Andrew Carnegie in the hope that the former ambassador's meeting with the Kaiser would further the cause of peace.

In the summer of 1912, Nellie took the girls and Roderick to Northeast Harbor for July and August; Charlemagne, Dominie and Geoffrey joined them in late August for a dinner Nellie had planned for seventy young people.

Roderick, who turned twenty that summer, had finished his first year at Harvard. He was a star athlete, a mediocre student and the most social of the Tower children. He was always in demand at dances and house parties in Boston, New

York and Philadelphia. The following year he would be invited to join the exclusive Porcelian Club at Harvard. Northeast Harbor suited him perfectly for the summer.

Young Helen had turned eighteen that June. She would have her debutante tea in Philadelphia in December of the following year. Nellie was laying the groundwork for her older daughter's official entrance into society in the prescribed manner: exposure at genteel gatherings of her peers and appropriate chaperonage at all times. Little did she know that Helen's coming out year would be eclipsed by a family scandal.

Early in January 1913, Helen and Gertrude returned to St.Timothy's. Dominie was to graduate from Yale in June, Geoffrey was in his third year at Yale and Roderick was a sophomore at Harvard.

Nellie hosted the annual meeting of the Equal Franchise Society on Saturday February 1, in the spacious gold room of the house on Locust Street. Peggy Shippen covered the event for the *Philadelphia Press*: "…the ladies seemed much elated over the success of the meeting…but then, people are always glad to go to Mrs. Tower's house. She is quite the leading hostess in the city…her own faculty of making you feel welcome and her reposeful hospitality have a charm all their own."

Charlemagne was absorbed in his work for the Carnegie Peace Endowment which held regular meetings in Washington. He and Nellie attended a reception at the Russian Embassy in Washington on February 10.

Suddenly in mid-February, rumors began to circulate that Dominie was secretly married. Nellie and Charlemagne were horrified. This was a serious charge because Yale undergraduates were not allowed to be married while at college; a secret marriage would mean expulsion.

On February 23, 1913, a story appeared in the *New York Tribune*:

CHARLEMAGNE TOWER, JR. TWO YEARS MARRIED

Philadelphia, Feb. 23—The identity of the mysterious wife of Charlemagne Tower, jr., a senior at Yale, and son of Charlemagne Tower, former Ambassador to Germany, probably will be revealed within the next twenty-four hours. State Senator Charles L. Brown, a widely known attorney, today acknowledged that he represented Mrs. Charlemagne Tower, jr.; that there really was such a person, and that she was the wife of the son of the former ambassador…This statement was made by Senator Brown immediately after ex-Ambassador Tower had denied that his son had been married. "I sent my son to college to be educated," said the former ambassador, "not to be married. I have communicated with him, and he told me he had no intention of taking such a step."

Senator Brown claimed that the marriage had taken place two years before and had been kept quiet so that Charlemagne jr. could graduate from Yale.

Dominie was quoted the same day in the *Philadelphia Public Ledger:* "There's nothing to it. I'm not married and that's all there is to it." Dominie did not graduate from Yale with his class in June, apparently for academic reasons, which added to the family's humiliation.

Nellie decided to take Roderick and the girls on a trip through the West. If nothing else, it would remove them from the family scandal. In July they began the long train trip west, first visiting Minnesota, then Yellowstone National Park and on to Vancouver before heading home.

After four nights on the train, Nellie and the three children reached the hotel in Yellowstone Park on July 10; Nellie wrote to Charlemagne who was at Waterville for the summer. "We have just had a family consultation and decided that we shall have to have a private carriage to go through the Park—we must pay extra for the privilege but the 'masses' are impossible."

In the fall the identity of Dominie's alleged wife was discovered—Georgeanna Burdick, a former musical comedy actress who had gone to New Haven with a touring company which closed, leaving her stranded. It was discovered that Georgeanna had been married previously to a man named Herman W. Allen whom she claimed to have divorced just before she supposedly married Charlemagne Tower, junior, whom she called "Chassie." She claimed that the wedding to Chassie took place on June 2, 1911, but no record of it could be found.

In October Dominie awaited the results of a special examination he had taken in September for a delayed diploma from Yale, but there was still the question of whether he was married or not. He was summoned to the dean's office where he again denied that he and Georgeanna Burdick were married.

The Towers were soon back in the headlines. *The New York Times* on October 10, 1913, ran the following story:

SON'S WIFE SUES EX-ENVOY TOWER

Philadelphia, Oct. 9—Charlemagne Tower, former Ambassador to Germany, is made defendant in a suit filed to-day by Mrs. Georgeanna Tower, asking damages for the alleged alienation of the affections of Charlemagne Tower, Jr., the 26-year-old [in fact Dominie was 24] son of the former diplomat, who, Mrs. Tower says, married her on June 7, 1911...Mrs. Tower was

Georgeanna Burdick, known among her friends by the name of "Dixie," because of her pronounced Southern accent.

The article went on to say that Georgeanna kept the marriage a secret because Yale undergraduates are not allowed to be married…"Chassie and I were married quietly," she said.

She told the *Times* that when she needed an operation, she went to Philadelphia to see Mr. Tower to ask for money: "Mr. Tower received me courteously, but afterward produced a paper, which he read to me, but would not let me read myself, and asked me to sign it. So far as I can remember he was virtually asking me to sign a statement to the effect that Chassie had never married me…"

Two days later, on October 12, the *New York Times* reported that Georgeanna Tower had been previously married in 1902 to Herman Allen and that she was 28 at the time of that wedding; when Allen was contacted he told the reporter that he and Georgeanna had divorced one week before she was to marry Tower. No record was found of the supposed marriage of Georgeanna and Dominie for June 7, 1913.

On November 19, 1913, *The New York Times* reported that Mrs. Georgeanna Burdick Tower was suing Charlemagne for "damages in excess of $200,000 for alleged alienation of the affections of his son…The amount of damages asked is said to be the largest ever filed in this city in a suit of this character."

Charlemagne was represented by ex-judge James Gay Gordon. Georgeanna hired Harry D. Wescott. The *Times* quoted Georgeanna:

> I am very sorry that all this has to come out. I did not want the notoriety that this suit will entail and I did not want to whip the Tower family. It is hard on Father and Mother Tower to have all of this come out at this time when they have daughters whose social debuts are near, but what else could I do?

The phrase "Father and Mother Tower" must have indeed rankled Nellie and Charlemagne. Georgeanna Burdick was now referred to by the newspapers as "Mrs. Charlemagne Tower Jr.," or "Young Mrs. Tower."

The timing of the scandal could not have been worse, as Georgeanna Burdick well knew. Helen's debutante parties would begin with a tea given by her parents on December 3 at their home at 1315 Locust Street. The *Philadelphia Press* of December 4 reported:

> HELEN SUSAN TOWER INTRODUCED AT TEA…One of the most important [teas of this season] was given by Mr. and Mrs. Charlemagne

Tower to introduce their daughter, Miss Helen Susan Tower, at their home…the large reception hall and drawing room were banked with flowers, baskets, ball chrysanthemums, roses, white lilacs…

Mrs. Tower wore a gown of soft white satin…a diamond collar and a necklace of pearls…the debutante had selected a girlish creation of white chiffon…trimmed with tiny pink roses.

Close to one thousand guests attended Helen's coming out ball on December 26, 1913, at Horticultural Hall. According to the *Philadelphia Press*, the vast hall was a riot of smilax, white lilies and hyacinths, contrasted with bright red azaleas and poinsettia. Supper was served at midnight.

Helen's coming out year was festive despite the pall cast by the Dominie-Dixie publicity. Friends of the family gave A New Year's Eve dinner-dance for her, and parties for all the debutantes of that year continued throughout the winter.

Charlemagne and Nellie had every reason to be hurt by Dominie's irresponsible behavior, and they were humiliated by the publicity. It is not known how much Charlemagne paid Georgeanna Burdick. The matter was finally dropped by the press.

Nellie and Charlemagne stuck by their wayward son with remarkable determination, always hoping that he would become more responsible. A job was found for him in the former Tower mining interests in Duluth, Minnesota. His lackluster college career was over at last.

In February, Charlemagne presided at the Peace and Arbitration Meeting held in Philadelphia on February 9, and resumed his speaking engagements.

Geoffrey graduated from Yale in June of 1914; in the fall, he would enter graduate school at Cornell University for a year's course in animal husbandry.

In the summer of 1914, the Towers again rented a house at Northeast Harbor. In August Helen visited the Vanderbilts in Newport, Rhode Island, for tennis week. Society columnist Peggy Shippen, writing in the *Philadelphia Press*, noted that young Helen's parties would continue all that year. "Moreover, she is in a fair way to getting the benefit of another debutante season; as her sister, Gertrude, is coming out next winter, and the two girls are so intimate that it will be like going out all over again for the elder sister…"

In Europe, a chain of events had started which would change the world. On June 28, 1914, Archduke Franz Ferdinand, the nephew and heir apparent of Franz Joseph, Emperor of Austria-Hungary, was assassinated at the Serbian capital of Sarajevo. In retribution, Franz Joseph delivered an unacceptable ultimatum to Serbia. That country appealed to Russia as protector of the Slavs and guarantor of Serbian independence.

Germany soon joined forces with Austria-Hungary against Serbia and Russia, and the First World War had started.

Having served in the American embassies of Austria-Hungary, Russia, and Germany, Charlemagne knew the principal players well, and he was well aware of the irreconcilable differences which existed among the diverse ethnic populations of the Balkans. When the war started he was not surprised, but he was deeply troubled. Over the next four years, he would watch the Europe that he had known disappear forever.

Helen Tower age 19 in 1913.

Gertrude Tower, age 17 in 1913.

Dominie Tower, at 24 in 1913

Geoffrey Tower at 23 in 1913

Roderick Tower at 21 in 1913.

21

Philadelphia 1915–1916 Family Tragedy

By early winter of 1915, the war in Europe was spreading rapidly. Germany had declared war on Russia and France, and had invaded Belgium. England had declared war on Germany.

America was officially neutral, and Charlemagne believed that the United States should remain neutral. His judgment was based on first hand observation of the forces which fueled the war—the constant unrest among the many ethnic factions which made up the empire of Austria-Hungary, the weakness of Russia under Nicholas II, and the Kaiser's paranoia toward England and France. It was a war waiting to happen, and that it had was no surprise to Charlemagne and other experienced diplomats.

During the first year of the war, life was changing for Americans in subtle ways. Nellie wrote to Geoffrey at Cornell on February 10, 1915: "Papa and I are well and busy although the season is not as gay as usual. We are glad that it is so and that all the fun comes to the dear debutante Gertrude, and also to Helen."

Charlemagne, in a letter to Geoffrey written a few weeks later, echoed the country's uncertainty about war when he told Geoffrey emphatically: "One thing is _very_ important; that is: let us know when you leave Ithaca, and where we could reach you at _any time_, if there should be need of it."

In the winter of 1915, when Germany blockaded Great Britain, some British merchant ships tried to escape German submarines by flying the flag of neutral America. Charlemagne was incensed. On February 23, 1915, he addressed the alumni of the University of Pennsylvania at its annual dinner at the Hotel Bellevue-Stratford. The *Evening Bulletin* of February 24 reported on the speech:

> "Hands off the flag," was the burden of a spirited address delivered last night by Charlemagne Tower, former Minister to Russia and Ambassador to Germany. "America should maintain an attitude of unyielding impartiality

toward all nations, insisting upon her right to traffic with all countries, whether belligerent or not"

Without naming either country he referred in the plainest manner to Germany's recent war-zone decree and warning to American shipping and to England's use of the American flag as a protection for her ocean commerce, insisting that both were invasions of American rights upon the seas.

[Mr. Tower said the flag is] "The highest emblem of our national existence...It must not be hoisted falsely on any foreign ship. It must not be trifled with by anyone."

It was a calm period in family life for the Towers. 1915 was Gertrude's debutante year; she and Helen were busy attending parties and doing the volunteer work expected of young women of the upper class. Roderick was a senior at Harvard and would attend Harvard Law School for the following year. Geoffrey felt that his course of study of animal husbandry at Cornell had real relevance to his future role as horse breeder.

Even Dominie, the black sheep of the family, had settled down. He had spent a year working in Duluth, Minnesota, devoting a good deal more concentration to his menial job than he ever had to his studies. On April 31, 1915, the *Philadelphia Evening Press* printed an article which no doubt originated in Charlemagne Tower's office in Philadelphia; it was a masterly job of public relations.

TOWER'S SON MAKES LIVING AS A LABORER

Advanced From Humble Job in Duluth to Engineer's Assistant at $3 a Day. Young Tower lives in a room at the Duluth Y.M.C.A...he has advanced himself from $2.20-a-day laborer in a steel furnace to $3-a-day engineer's assistant. In this advancement, his course of study in the Sheffield Scientific School at Yale stood him in good stead...
Through it all, however, the young man was careful not to boast of his family connection and referred to it only when questioned.

The end of the Dominie-Dixie story came in June 1915, when Georgeanna Burdick Tower was granted a divorce from Dominie; the grounds were not made public but it can be assumed that it was desertion. The whole affair, which had gone on for four years, had cost the Towers considerable distress as well as untold thousands of dollars in legal fees and settlements.

In the summer of 1915, Nellie went to California to visit family and friends. While staying with her sister, Ada, in San Diego in July, she was quoted in the national press in a strong defense of the Kaiser[1]:

MRS. TOWER DEFENDS KAISER

Mrs. Charlemagne Tower…who with her husband enjoyed the friendship of the Emperor William…told reporters that the Kaiser, in adopting deadly gases and the like did so because the Allies forced him to by [using] similar methods.

"The Kaiser is a very great man," Mrs. Tower said. "He would make a sacrifice for the good of his people…his associates in Germany are being misjudged by Americans. I have the most intense feeling of patriotism for my own country, but this does not prevent me from doing justice to the German people and the Emperor, who is merely doing everything possible to save his country in a war which was precipitated by the Allies."

These were ill chosen remarks, to say the least. Nellie's loyalty to the Kaiser was unshaken by the events of the war in Europe. On August 8, she was featured in a society story in the *San Francisco Chronicle*:

MRS. CHARLEMAGNE TOWER, "VON MOLTKE OF SOCIETY" RETURNS TO SAN FRANCISCO

Bringing with her reminiscences of early social life in California, where she was born, and more recent memories of brilliant court functions in the great capitals of Europe, Mrs. Charlemagne Tower, wife of the former American Ambassador to Berlin, is once more back in San Francisco and the central figure in a round of social activities.

Mrs. Tower's established reputation for years as the leader of court society in the great German capital, together with her gracious tact, her brilliancy as a conversationalist, and the rare polish she has attained through intimate contact with those of the highest diplomatic circles, has made her return to San Francisco society most welcome…it was in Berlin that she gained the greatest recognition, and was referred to by the Kaiser as "the von Moltke…of society…the greatest social leader of my reign…"

On February 23, 1916, Charlemagne was praised in an editorial in the Philadelphia *Ledger* for his views on the war in Europe, expressed in a recent speech. The editorial noted that the former ambassador advocated that America not plan for war but plan to prevent war; not arm and equip with the thought of war but

---

1.   Quoted on July 20, 1915—name of newspaper is missing from clipping.

with the thought of minimizing the danger of war…The editorial quoted Charlemagne: "For forty years Europe has been planning for this war…Sentiment plays no part in international relations; they are based entirely upon community of interest, and it is well within the bounds of probability that what has occurred before in the world may happen again, and that the opponent of today may be fighting as allies, side by side, within the present or next generation."

While working in Duluth, Dominie had fallen in love with Barbara Rupley, whom Nellie and Charlemagne had met in Berlin when Barbara, as a young girl, spent three years in the German capital studying music.

Barbara was both musically talented and lovely looking. Her family were solid mid-westerners and Nellie and Charlemagne agreed, no doubt with a sense of relief, that she would make a very good wife for their once wayward son. Dominie and Barbara were already engaged when she visited the Tower family in Philadelphia in May of 1916.

It was during Barbara's visit, on May 13, that a tragedy struck the Tower family that completely overshadowed their former anguish over Dominie's indiscretions. Their youngest daughter, Gertrude, was fatally injured in an automobile accident while returning from a party.

Gertrude was nineteen years old that spring and Helen was twenty-one. The family chauffeur had driven them to a dance, one of the countless parties of Gertrude's debutante year. Helen drove home with the chauffeur, but Gertrude begged to ride with a young man named Dougherty who had a new sports car. Helen, who had been cautioned by Nellie to keep an eye on her younger sister, agreed to let her sister ride with Dougherty, providing she and the chauffeur followed them home.

Young Dougherty, thrilled with the power of his new sports car, began taking the curves in Fairmount Park too fast. When a park guard attempted to stop him, he simply drove faster. Suddenly he lost control of the car and ran off the road. The car turned over, throwing him fifteen feet away, but pinning Gertrude underneath. Dougherty recovered but Gertrude never regained consciousness. Four days later, she died from internal injuries.

Nellie and Charlemagne were devastated. It was every parent's nightmare. After they had protected their daughters so carefully, worried about them when they were away from them, crossed the Atlantic many times, lived in foreign countries, and then to have their youngest child snatched from them because a young man was showing off with his new car was almost too much to bear.

Helen felt completely responsible. Every day of her life thereafter she blamed herself for not saying "no" to her sister and making her go home with her in the family car. No matter how her parents tried to ease her guilt, she slipped into a depression from which nothing would rouse her.

The Tower family went together to Waterville to bury Gertrude in the Tower plot in the Waterville cemetery. Dominie wrote to his fiancée, Barbara, who had returned home after the accident. He described the mood of desolation at the Homestead: "I feel as though the bottom had suddenly dropped out of everything…"

During the summer of 1916, Nellie found little that could provide solace. Helen's depression deepened. Her parents soon realized that Waterville held too many memories of Gertrude. Finally, at Charlemagne's insistence, Nellie took her daughter to Maine where they stayed at the Kimball House in Northeast Harbor in late July where Charlemagne would join them in August. On July 17, Charlemagne wrote to Nellie in Maine; the letter was later placed among her most treasured possessions with "<u>Save Always</u>" written across the envelope.

> July 17, 1916
> Waterville
> My dear Nennie,
>   …I have been anxious ever since you left here about your feelings at the return to a place so full of associations and crowded with the familiar sights and sounds of days that were filled with happiness. I see that it has not been an easy task. And yet, I am convinced that it is best both for you and Helen to have this opportunity to come into contact with people again. I think you will feel this yourself as the time goes on…
>   We cannot avoid now every association that recalls happiness, for that would bar the sweetest memories of our lives. We must think of them with the sweetness that they gave, not with grief alone, because that would embitter what is left to us, and we <u>must go on!</u> For it is not the pain and bitterness of sorrow, but the sweet and loving memory that we must cherish. This is what our flowers mean that are picked and brought with loving hands.
>   If you were here at this moment you could not sufficiently rise out of yourself, for the surroundings afford but little present help…I am confident that you will find kindness all about you, and I trust that you will meet friends constantly, from day to day, who will somewhat add interest to your life…
>   Here at the Homestead everything is going along as usual, with nothing new to report…
>   I shall write to you again tomorrow, and…I hope to hear from you again tomorrow also.
> Your affectionate Husband,
> Charlemagne Tower

In the envelope with Charlemagne's letter, was this poem by James Whitcomb Riley:

Away
I cannot say,
And will not say
That she is dead.
She is just away!
With a cheery smile
And a wave of the hand
She has wandered into an unknown land
And left us dreaming how very fair
It needs must be, since she lingers there,
And you—oh you, who the wildest yearn
For the old-time step and the glad return
Think of her faring on, as dear
In the love of There, as the love of Here.
Think of her still as the same, I say,
She is not dead—she is just away.

In the summer of 1916, Roderick signed up for aviation school at Mineola, Long Island.

That fall the Towers did not renew the lease on the Locust Street house. They would make Waterville their home and travel at other times. When they were in Philadelphia, they would stay at a hotel.

22

Philadelphia 1917–1918
Mourning

On January 10, 1917, Dominie married Barbara Rupley at a ceremony in Duluth, Minnesota. Nellie, Helen and Geoffrey attended the wedding, but Charlemagne did not, probably due to the bronchial trouble that plagued him in winter. Roderick could not get leave from flight school to attend the wedding.

Nellie wrote Charlemagne from the Spalding Hotel as soon as she arrived in Duluth:

> January 9
> Dearest Charlemagne,
>   Mr. Rupley and Dominie were at the station at 8:30 o'clock and Barbara came to see us when we fixed the hour, 11 o'clock. In her hand she had some flowers for our darling's [Gertrude's] picture and some wedding cake to taste. We lunched with her mother and then saw the presents.
>   Their home is extremely refined, tasteful and attractive. The lunch was delicious and everything made an excellent impression upon us all.
>   You will be glad to hear that lots of our friends have sent presents, suitable, tasteful and exactly right…I will write you again tomorrow.
>   Your devoted,
>   Nennie,

Dominie's time of exile was over; he and Barbara moved back to Philadelphia where he worked for the Pennsylvania Railroad Company. They leased a house on Mannheim Street in Germantown.

The United States was drawing closer to the war in Europe. On January 31, 1917, Germany notified the United States that unrestricted submarine warfare would commence the next day. The United States severed relations with Germany, but it was not until after German submarines sunk three homebound

American ships on March 16 and 17, 1917, that the United States officially declared war on Germany.

Geoffrey enlisted in the Army and was commissioned second lieutenant in the Remount Service that supplied horses and mules for the military.[1]

Nellie, Charlemagne and Helen went to San Diego to visit Nellie's sister, Ada, in April. In the April 28, 1917 edition of *The Californian Magazine*, Charlemagne was pictured on the cover and quoted:

> "There is only one thing for every loyal American to say and one thing for him to do, in the situation in which the country finds itself today: that is, to support the Government of the United States in every way and with all his strength.
>
> "Our plain duty is, to follow the leadership of the President and to sustain the authority of Congress in every step that they may take for the honor of the nation."

The magazine article continued:

> This famous diplomat and his wife have given their youngest son, Roderick Tower, to the most dangerous branch of the service in the U.S. Army. Young Mr. Tower, age twenty-three, brilliant and promising, has recently enlisted in the aviation corps and is in training at Mineola. His position with the Pierpont Morgan Co. of New York City will be saved for him while he is engaged in this hazardous work for his country.

This kind of publicity helped offset the criticism Nellie and Charlemagne felt from others about their friendship with the Kaiser, and Charlemagne's advocacy, in the early years of the war, of American neutrality.

Writing to his father on May 1, Roderick described his flying lessons: "The regular course comprises going up every day for 30 minutes with an instructor till one is good enough to go alone. Then a total of 20 hours alone is required, after which comes the test."

As the first anniversary of Gertrude's death drew near, Roderick marked the sad occasion with a letter to his mother, written on May 16:

> I have been thinking for many weeks of the significance of tomorrow, May 17th, and have arranged with Geoff for him to wire you our love in the morn-

---

1.   Well over one million horses and mules were employed by the Remount in World War I; an estimated 63,000 of them were killed during the war.

ing…it was one year ago tomorrow that we all met at 1315 for the saddest thing in our lives and never has a day passed in that year that we haven't all thought of that wonderful little sister.

In the same letter Roderick attempted to reassure his mother about the safety of flying:

"They do not plan to have a single accident at Mineola this summer, as every plane has been carefully devised and everything most thoroughly done to see to this."

From San Diego, Nellie and Helen went north to Lake Tahoe where they stayed while Charlemagne went back to Waterville. Nellie tried hard to keep moving to provide new surroundings for Helen who was still deeply depressed. Above all, Nellie tried to avoid places that were strongly associated with Gertrude. Waterville, of course, could not be avoided. It was now their only home and for Nellie it had taken on a new meaning— it was the final resting place for her beloved youngest child, in a grave marked with a small marble cross wreathed in a vine of marble roses.

Nellie stayed at Tahoe until the middle of June when she decided that she and Helen were strong enough to go to Waterville again. She was comforted knowing that Hester Webb, having supervised the opening of the house, would stay on to lend emotional support to the family.

That summer, a full compliment of new servants had been hired for the house in Waterville. Since the closing of the house in Philadelphia, there was no longer a permanent staff of servants who could accompany the family north for the summer, except Albert Spengel.

Charlemagne arrived in Waterville on June 22, 1917. He wrote Nellie at Lake Tahoe immediately:

> Jennings and Mrs. Jennings were here awaiting me, smiling and proud of the place now in order. It looks very fresh and beautiful, though the garden is just beginning. We shall have strawberries by the time you come, but the only thing at present is the asparagus, which is excellent. It is quite wonderful that we could have replanned the whole system here, with new people and all, and yet be able to have it move off smoothly from the start. The house is running today as if nothing had happened.
>
> Hester appears to have done remarkably well…Old Maggie, the laundress, is here, evidently very glad to be in her old place; as for the work that Charles did about the house and in the garden, Albert has brought a man with him from the Union League.

The cross at the little grave is very beautiful and I think that you will be satisfied with it; a pure white piece of marble, the two roses are beautifully chiseled on the side…In the autumn when the leaves are gone, we shall see it plainly from the windows of the Homestead, but not now…

I think you have decided wisely to come home. It is quiet…but it is your own and I believe that in the long run you will feel contented with your decision, and fortified.

The next day, June 23, Charlemagne again wrote to Nellie. His solicitude gives an insight into their loving relationship:

This morning I picked the first roses, so that now the picture of little Trudy on your writing desk is surrounded again by flowers…The weather is bright and pleasant since I have been here, after very cold and disagreeable storms…The dogs are well; Leo has grown very strong…Flockie [from Berlin days] looks much better than last year; and he made a really complimentary fuss over my arrival, night before last…In the house, everything goes along comfortably and well with the new regime and the new servants.

The cook is a mature, pleasant faced Dane who evidently likes the surroundings and is sending for her sister as kitchen maid; our food is like what we used to have in Rittenhouse Square…The other two women are Swedes. One, the waitress, is tall and bony…the chambermaid is shorter and younger with round spectacles…

Grace Putnam's family will not arrive until after you do, for which I am glad. I would much rather have you established first.

Nellie and Helen stayed at the Homestead until late August. As her parents had feared, Helen's depression deepened in Waterville, where she and Gertrude had always been together. In late August Nellie took her to Newport, Rhode Island, where they stayed at the Muenchinger-King Hotel for several weeks.

Nellie, who was growing desperate in her attempts to divert her daughter, decided that possibly Helen's friend, Marguerite Caperton, might be the answer. If only Helen could be with people her age, her mother reasoned, her depression might lift.

Marguerite Caperton, who was extremely attractive and popular with other young people, was staying in Newport. She was the daughter of Rear Admiral William B. Caperton, U.S.N., Commander of the Pacific Fleet. Helen had visited the Caperton family in Cuba the previous spring at Nellie's insistence.

Nellie wrote to Charlemagne on August 14, giving him news of their old friends. She and Nellie had lunched with Mrs. Vanderbilt earlier that day: "Although there were no young people at all Helen appeared extremely well…this is one of the only places where our darling Gertrude never has been and yet I think of her as always as lying so close to my heart…"

Nellie found herself in an awkward position socially. The Towers' admiration for the Kaiser was now viewed with suspicion. Nellie wrote Charlemagne:

> The feeling here is unpleasant when [the war] is discussed so I hope to keep away from society at large…I could be fairly contented here if Helen were having gaiety but she is not. Marguerite is a very lovely girl but she has many beaux at her door every moment. She is on the fly continually and with the best intentions toward Nellie cannot drag her along…
>
> I am not ready to…start home. I had hoped to have Helen meet some young people at Mrs. Vanderbilt's but that failed…she is calm…very different from her attitude in Waterville, but I am constantly wondering why I am here…

Nellie wrote that Helen finally did team up with a group of young people one evening, "to see the troops start off for France…it made Helen so very sad, just as I warned her in advance."

In the end, Nellie acknowledged that the trip to Newport was a dismal failure. She and Helen returned to Waterville for the rest of the summer.

In the winter of 1918, Roderick, called Rod by everyone except his parents, was a flying instructor stationed at Call Field in Wichita Falls, Texas. Nellie and Charlemagne were enormously proud of him, although his letters must have caused concern for his safety. He told his mother in a letter written on January 14: "My students are coming along excellently, and I now take them over on to the Standard machines to finish them off and set them loose."

Rod loved flying and enjoyed instructing new cadets. His enthusiasm was even greater in a letter to his mother written on February 12:

> As I wrote you last Saturday, I am in charge of the cadets' cross country work here, and today I took them off for their first trip away from the Field and I have mapped out carefully the whole thing, even to the point of going out in an auto, and selecting suitable places for them to land. This certainly is great fun, and they will like it a lot.
>
> This morning a cadet fell in a spin about 1200 ft. into a tree, and although he smashed the Curtiss all to pieces, he only scratched his nose. We had a hard time finding him, or the machine, but finally the little feller came running in and, standing at attention, said to the Flying Major, "Sir, Cadet (I don't remember his name) reports that he has fallen, and wishes a new machine—preferably a Standard this time!!!" I certainly like that spirit….

By the summer of 1918, Helen's depression had lifted, and she sought ways to take part in the war effort. She enrolled in both a first aid course and a secretarial class in Washington, where Nellie and Helen shared a suite of rooms at a hotel.

That summer Helen met Army Major William Abbott Robertson, who had recently returned from a year's tour of duty in France. He was strikingly handsome, with the quiet good manners of a southern gentleman.

In October, Rod was back in Mineola, Long Island, teaching flying and serving as head of his squadron. On October 13, 1918 he wrote to his father: "Influenza and pneumonia are pretty bad with us, though not nearly as bad as at [Fort] Meade and [Fort] Devens. I have 15 enlisted men with the [influenza]^2 and one officer died today of pneumonia.... We are to go overseas in December, some say, and others say not till February.".

Rod did not go overseas because the Armistice was declared on November 11, 1918. Geoffrey had already arrived in France. The allied victory was bittersweet—the cost of the war in human life took away any thought of rejoicing. The world was stunned by the devastation of this new kind of mechanized war that claimed an estimated fifteen million lives.

In the space of four years, the war had put an end to the world Charlemagne and Nellie had known. The vast empire of Austria-Hungary was no more. Emperor Francis Joseph, who died early in the war at age 86, did not live to witness the dissolution of his empire.

Nellie and Charlemagne had barely been able to grasp the horror of the massacre of Tsar Nicholas, the Tsarina Alexandra, and their five children in July 1918, at Ekaterinburg, during the Russian Revolution. When the Towers had visited the royal family in the Crimea sixteen years earlier, Nicholas and Alexandra had three pretty little daughters; the arrival of a fourth daughter and later the longed-for heir, Tsarevich Alexi, lay in the future, as did the terrible consequences of the boy's hemophilia.

The German Empire was now in shambles, the Kaiser a fugitive. A number of the Towers' German friends had been killed, others lived in disgrace.

Being a diplomat and statesman, as well as a student of history, Charlemagne took the long view of the events in Europe. We can safely assume that he recoiled at the harsh and unreasonable terms of the Treaty of Versailles, and he may well

---

2.   The Spanish flu pandemic of 1918 killed 500,000 Americans and between 20 million and 50 million people worldwide. It is estimated that 80 percent of the total number of battle deaths during World War I were from influenza.

have predicted the effect these severe measures would have on the future of Europe.

Geoffrey was the only member of the Tower family who was in Europe in the immediate aftermath of World War I. On November 15, 1918, Charlemagne wrote to his son in care of the Auxiliary Remount Depot 345, American Expeditionary Forces:

> We were all made happy a few days ago by the receipt of your Postal-card announcing your safe arrival overseas, which we had been hoping for by every mail for nearly a week. I sent the good news at once to Mamma and Helen, Dominie and Barbara, and Hester and Roderick. I received the letter that you wrote me the night that you embarked, with your requests which I have carried out…
>
> I have no doubt that Mamma gave you in her letters all the news of the family. I am happy to say that we are all well. Roderick had his orders for overseas in his pocket and was ready to embark, when word arrived of the Armistice. He is still at the Camp at Garden City, though I doubt whether he will be sent abroad now. Mamma and Helen are in Washington where Helen took up her post as Assistant to Miss Boardman in The Red Cross. She has given great satisfaction for she was thoroughly trained, as you know, through the summer.
>
> We shall be looking for your letter with the greatest interest, especially to hear how you are, how your voyage was and what your impressions are at being in France once more. Let us hear from you whenever you can…
>
> I hope that your service abroad will be successful and filled with interest for the rest of your life. We shall gladly welcome you when you come home…

On November 17, 1918, Helen wrote to her brother Geoffrey from Washington:

> Dearest Geoffrey,
>
> You seem so far away and we all miss you very, very much, but you are so constantly in our thoughts and I am sure you must be having a mighty interesting time and wonderful experiences over there. It is hard, in fact almost impossible, to believe that war is really over! It will be so nice to get your first letters.
>
> Well, Mama has written you the news of my engagement to Major Robertson, so I wanted to add a few lines to tell you myself how very, very happy I am, and how I wish you were here to share it with me, and to know "Robby." The whole family is crazy about him, especially Rod, and I know you will be too. We don't expect to write our friends or to announce it until Xmas, and then probably get married later in the winter in Philadelphia.

I love my work as secretary and then I can see Robby every day, so it is ideal being here, and Mama and I have such nice rooms at the Hotel. Papa comes for week-ends and whenever he can. We expect to all spend Thanksgiving in Baltimore with Dominie and Barbara in their cute home. Robby and I will probably motor up—he has a little Buick in which we motor about and have lots of fun!

Mama probably wrote you that Rod flew down here to say "goodbye" the day Armistice was declared, and it certainly was exciting! It must be pretty hard for him not knowing what to expect next, in a way.

Well, that is all the news. I don't get much time to write as I go to the office from 9:30 to about 4, coming home for lunch. But I love it. So much love to you, Geoff, and best luck in your work.

Your honeysis, Helen

Helen Susan Tower and Major William Abbott Robertson were married in Philadelphia on December 21, 1918, at Holy Trinity Church. In the photograph of the wedding party published in the *Public Ledger* of December 22, an unsmiling bride and her handsome groom are surrounded by their wedding party—seven bridesmaids, including several Tower cousins and the dazzling Marguerite Caperton, and seven officers in dress military uniforms sitting cross-legged on the floor in front.

Helen's happiness with Robby delighted her parents. The bride and the groom, who had just been awarded the Legion of Honor by the French government, moved to San Diego where he continued his career in the Army.

In February 1919 Helen told her parents the joyous news that she and Robby were expecting a baby due in October. Nothing could have pleased them more. "The Major," as they referred to Robby, was turning out to be the perfect son-in-law.

Geoffrey wrote to Dominie from France in the spring of 1919; the letter is undated but would have been written in April:

Remount Depot # 21
A.P.O. # 727
Dear Dom,

Things have certainly changed in the Tower family in the last 12 months, and all the changes have been good ones and we should consider ourselves lucky. Helen married, Rod in N.Y. again, and me over here—we could not have foretold [any of it] a year ago at this time! Well, I think the nightmare...is gone forever from the face of the earth and it showed the American people to be self-sacrificing and generous to a degree, with <u>no material</u> ends to gain in the war. By the way, you ought to see how well some of the people have lived over here during the entire war, and all through the worst and best periods of the war the wine and liquor traffic was going apace right in this country. Booze raised on a <u>big</u> scale instead of wheat. The liquor fiend has sure got the country by the throat...

It is very gratifying to know how heartily you are all back of me in being over here, and though we arrived too late for any hero-stuff in the main arena, it was not our fault and we didn't know how things would come out. Ours was the last group of squadrons to leave Jacksonville and many officers who were still there at that time are now mustered out of the service...

The happiness that Helen has now is a great source of happiness to me and I know how you all feel about it too. Also I am glad Rod is out of the air service and hope he will work into something satisfactory in New York...

There is no telling how long we will still be over here and I know there is no fair means to hasten matters. The returning troops have mostly been over here for some time, and we are now busy receiving horses from returning organizations and selling them to the French...

23

End of An Era 1919–1923

Geoffrey returned to the United States in May 1919, and was mustered out of the service in June. He planned to support himself in the horse business.

For Nellie and Charlemagne, Geoffrey's return brought a great sense of relief. Even though the actual fighting was over, there was always danger in a country recently torn by war. Nellie and Charlemagne settled down to enjoy their adult children, and help them when they saw the need.

In October 1919, Nellie went to San Diego to be with her daughter Helen for the birth of her first baby. William Abbott Robertson Jr. was born on October 18.

In late October, Rod proposed to Flora Payne Whitney, the daughter of Gertrude Vanderbilt Whitney, the well-known sculptor, and Harry Payne Whitney. Flora, a petite, dark-haired, beauty, had been engaged to a friend of Rod's, Quentin Roosevelt, Theodore Roosevelt's youngest son. When Quentin, a flier, was shot down and killed over France on July 14,1918, Flora was broken hearted. It was natural for her to be comforted by the friendship of Rod Tower, also a flier, and a friend of Quentin's.

Flora and Rod's engagement was announced by her family in February of 1920. The wedding took place at St. Bartholomew's Church on Monday, April 19 at 4 o'clock in the afternoon. Flora's mother had directed the decorating of the church, creating a striking art nouveau effect with trees made of white Easter lilies.

Geoffrey was Rod's best man. Instead of bridesmaids, Flora's attendants were the children of relatives. Close to a thousand guests attended the reception at the Whitney home at 971 Fifth Avenue, after which Flora and Rod left on their honeymoon trip to Hawaii.

For Nellie and Charlemagne, Rod's marriage into a family of wealth and distinction must have been very satisfying. They knew Alice Vanderbilt, Flora's grandmother, from Newport, and Alice's daughter, Gladys, Flora's aunt, had stayed with the Towers at the Embassy in Berlin in the winter of 1907 when she fell in love with her future husband, Count Szechenyi. Now Gladys's three little daughters were in the wedding party.

As she sat in St. Bartholomew's, Nellie may well have reflected that this was the kind of wedding which she had envisioned for all of her children, and especially her daughters—a connection with a well-known, wealthy old family from New York, Philadelphia or Boston.

It was not surprising that Roderick would have a society wedding. As a bachelor, during his college years and afterwards, the handsome Rod Tower loved society and society loved him. With his elegant manners and quick wit, he fit in anywhere. He was not shy as were his two older brothers, and his enthusiasm and vitality were infectious. Since the war, he was known as a flying ace, which made him even more attractive to his peers.

Rod was clearly very much in love with Flora, and Nellie and Charlemagne were happy for him. They may not have known how much in love Flora had been with Quentin Roosevelt, and that it might be too soon for her to make another commitment.

Life was very different for Nellie now that Helen was living in California. She and her daughter had been together constantly after the death of Gertrude, and Nellie had come to rely on that closeness in coping with her own grief.

Increasingly Nellie found the tenets of Theosophy, especially the belief in reincarnation and transmigration of the soul, a comfort in coming to terms with her loss. Nellie would practice and study Theosophy through meetings and readings for the rest of her life.

Nellie was never idle. She performed good works where she saw a need, both among her friends and in the larger community, just as she had when she was a young woman in Oakland. She also shared Charlemagne's interest in politics. She had been an active supporter of women's suffrage, which culminated in the passage of the Nineteenth Amendment in 1920.

On October 20, 1920, Nellie addressed members of the ways and means committee of the Republican national committee for Pennsylvania, on "Why I Am a Republican." On October 25, she spoke before the same group in favor of Charlemagne's mentor, Boies Penrose, who was seeking re-election to the United States Senate. She cited Penrose as "one of the ablest statesmen in the United States Senate, and one of Pennsylvania's most distinguished sons…"

Shortly after their wedding, Rod and Flora had moved to Los Angeles where Rod worked in a training program with the General Petroleum Company. His work schedule made married life difficult for Flora and him, and social life impossible.

On February 22, 1921 Rod wrote to his mother giving her a grim picture of their life in Los Angeles:

> Today is a holiday for me, and I believe that tomorrow I shall be changed again at the Refinery, taking on the arduous duties of a fireman at the Stills. This should prove instructive, although after a while it will be very hard, as it calls for shift work—or working all night.
>
> The picture of how our days and evenings are spent is not very complex. I start off very early in the a.m. in my motor for Vernon, 6 1/2 miles distant, and spend the day there. Flora then has her motor and chauffeur, this charming house, and the whole day before her. I must say she puts it in well and wisely, though most quietly and no lost energy due to excitement or nervous tantrums. She reads a good deal, sees a few lady friends who are all older.
>
> Evening entertainments of and in Society we have not touched much, nor hardly grazed. I cannot possibly stay up late at night after a tedious day and with another and still another staring me in the face, and so we have just not gone to most of the things we have been invited to, and they haven't been so many, as after all we are much younger than most of them out here.

In December of 1921, Flora and Rod had a baby girl, Pamela, born in Los Angeles.

Geoffrey had leased a farm in Port Chester, New York, for his horse business. Hester and George Webb were helping him settle into his bachelor quarters. Hester would keep house for Geoffrey and George would help with the horses. Money was very tight, Geoffrey told his mother in a letter of May 4, 1922, and he was looking forward to his monthly allowance check of $200 from his father.

In May 1922, Charlemagne had a relapse of his bronchial problems that became so severe that he was hospitalized for five days at the Pennsylvania Hospital in Philadelphia. Afterwards, he and Nellie spent a quiet summer at Waterville. In August, Helen, Robby and their little son, Bobbie, were visiting from California when Robby came down with influenza, causing the entire household in Waterville to be placed in quarantine.

On September 18 Nellie wrote to Geoffrey at his horse farm at Port Chester:

> Dearest Geoffrey,
>
> I was so pleased to have your letter on Saturday and to know that you may come here next Sunday.
>
> Robby is improving now very fast—today he walked about the grounds. Unfortunately, however, he is still isolated because the daily examination of

the culture taken at the laboratory in Albany according to state law, still shows the presence of bacteria.

We are therefore still in quarantine, can go nowhere and see no one. Each day the Doctor hopes to get the good news of its being alright but until then we must keep on with all the precautions we are using now.

In this case, you must not come up Sunday but I will write or telegraph by Friday so that you will know the outcome.

I can see that once Robby is able to come downstairs for his meals and go about naturally he would very soon have his normal strength, but the doctor says there are cases occasionally which last for weeks before the infection is entirely gone—this would be a calamity although at present everyone is very patient and all is going well....
Fondly,

Mother

On September 30, 1922, Charlemagne wrote Geoffrey from Waterville to alert him that Robby was still in quarantine:

The Major [Robby] is up and out on horse back every day, apparently as well as he ever was, but Dr. Randall has not been able as yet to release us because the reports from the laboratory which come every day are still indicative of the presence of the germs of diphtheria and consequently we are obliged to keep to the house. This is an inconvenience of course, and we are hoping from day to day for a turn in affairs.

In the meantime, our family life goes on exactly as usual...
Your affectionate Father,
Charlemagne Tower

As they grew older, the routine of summers in Waterville suited Nellie and Charlemagne well. In September 1922, Nellie would be 64 years old; Charlemagne was 74. They no longer went to Northeast Harbor. Their children, and now their grandchildren, could visit them at the Homestead and experience the same pleasures of country life which Charlemagne and his father before him had enjoyed as children.

Charlemagne and Nellie left Waterville in November 1922 to spend the winter at Green Hills Farm Hotel in Overbrook, in suburban Philadelphia. Charlemagne was not well.

In January 1923, he was admitted to Pennsylvania Hospital with pneumonia. Two weeks later he was no better. Nellie stayed with him constantly. The children gathered at Charlemagne's bedside. He died in his sleep on February 24, 1923, at the age of seventy-five. *The New York Times*, February 24, 1923, stated:

Mr. Tower's diplomatic career was particularly brilliant...[after serving as Minister Plenipotentiary in Vienna] it was at the court of the Tsar that Mr. Tower endeavored to bring the American Embassy to a level with those of the other great powers in the matter of display as well as diplomacy...

In 1902, when Mr. Tower was sent to Berlin by President Roosevelt, began the most brilliant period of his diplomatic career. For the six years of his term as Ambassador to Germany he earned and kept the proverbially fickle William as his friend...when Ambassador Tower made known his intention to resign, the Kaiser did his utmost to dissuade him.

[Mr. Tower was] a trustee for the University of Pennsylvania, Colgate University and Hamilton College; a member of the board of City Trust of Philadelphia, the Academy of Natural Sciences, the American Philosophical Society and the American Institute of Mining Engineers...and was President of the Historical Society of Pennsylvania.

Mr. Tower was also a Director in the Philadelphia and Reading Coal and Iron Company, the Lehigh Coal and Navigation Company; the New York, New Haven & Hartford Railroad Company and the Pennsylvania Steel Company.

The various obituaries failed to mention one affiliation that was especially important to Charlemagne: he was one of twenty-eight founding members of the Carnegie Endowment for International Peace.

Charlemagne's diplomatic career was indeed impressive. As a statesman, he was respected as an adept negotiator: in Vienna, he reassured Emperor Franz Joseph whose sympathies lay with Spain during the Spanish-American War. Charlemagne encouraged Secretary of State John Hay to push a bill through Congress exempting naturalized Austrians from military service.

When he served as Ambassador to Russia, Charlemagne was successful in compelling the Russians to accept arbitration for eight-year-old claims against them for seizing American whaling ships in the Bering Sea.

Finally, as Ambassador to Germany, Charlemagne succeeded in calming the often mercurial Kaiser, especially when the monarch was in a panic over the total defeat of the Russian fleet after the battle of Tsushima in May 1905, during the Russo-Japanese War; the Kaiser worried that the riots which would ensue in Russia could spread and threaten monarchies throughout Europe. He wanted Charlemagne to urge President Theodore Roosevelt to mediate a peace settlement between Japan and Russia to end hostilities, and in the end, the President did.

Charlemagne brought to the diplomatic service a level of excellence unusual under the American system of using ambassadorships as political paybacks and rewards for campaign contributions. Seldom was a diplomat better equipped by education and background than Charlemagne. Nor was an ambassador's wife better suited to the role of international hostess than was Nellie.

A tribute to Charlemagne from the October 14, 1907 *Bradford Daily* in Pennsylvania at the time of his announced retirement well expresses Charlemagne's success as a diplomat:

> The ambassador's tact and energy made him the foremost American ambassador abroad...he established closer relations between our country and Germany, politically, socially and commercially, and his personality stood out clearly among our representatives abroad as our ablest and most popular diplomat...The American people are quick to appreciate their permanent benefactors and with one accord they have placed in their hall of fame the Honorable Charlemagne Tower.

The brilliance and success of the diplomatic years lay in stark contrast to the disappointments that came later. When they returned to Philadelphia, Nellie and Charlemagne found that their three sons, though closer to them geographically, were difficult to bring back into the fold. The scandal of Dominie's secret marriage to Georgeanna tarnished the family name and caused Nellie and Charlemagne great humiliation. The years of lavish entertaining abroad had considerably eroded Charlemagne's personal fortune as did the law suit brought against Charlemagne by Georgeanna Burdick.

The war in Europe destroyed the life of the glittering royal courts and proved the futility of the peace efforts at which Charlemagne had worked during his years as a diplomat. In the middle of the war came the ultimate personal tragedy for Nellie and Charlemagne, in the death of their youngest daughter.

Charlemagne Tower
1848–1923

24

Nellie Tower Widow 1923–1931

Charlemagne left a small estate valued at $25,000. Years of public service and an extravagant style of living had depleted his private fortune. The Federal income tax, instituted in 1913, also took its toll. Nellie and their children, however, would be provided for under the terms of Charlemagne's father's trust.

Nellie would receive a fourth share of what her husband had received annually during his life; the four children would have equal shares in three-fourths of Charlemagne's share of his father's estate.

When Charlemagne died, Nellie knew that she would no longer have a generous income, but she could not have guessed just how frugal she would have to be.

In April of 1923, she arranged for the auction of Charlemagne's vast library as well as a good many of the rugs, furniture and art objects that had been in storage in Philadelphia.

In late May, when the snow and frozen ground had melted, Charlemagne's remains were removed from the mausoleum in Philadelphia where they had been temporarily placed at his death, and taken to Waterville for burial in the family cemetery.

Rod, who was aboard the Sinclair Navigation Company's oil tanker, *S.S. Wm. B. Thompson* at sea, was unable to attend his father's interment in Waterville. He wrote to his mother on May 24:

> My very dear Mother:
>
> I write you this line with the profoundest emotion and my heart is with you in the very greatest sympathy of which I am capable. I have been thinking of the sad little family group in Waterville every minute for many hours and I figure that at this very moment the service is going forward in the cemetery on the hillside and that you are all saying one final farewell to all that is mortal of our dear Father.
>
> You have had such courage, dear Mother, and have shown in the last 4 months, such an unflinching, magnificent spirit and not only will it always be a divine example of fortitude to any of us in the future…but I feel sure that it

also will prove itself a gratification to you to have been so fine and so great. And, with God's blessing on you forever, may the rest of your stay on the Earth be filled with many joys and may your life be as full as possible.

I shall think of you very often and shall be hoping that the complete change of every thing you are starting out upon will benefit you in a thousand ways and bring you lots of satisfaction.

With lots of love and all good wishes—adieu

Your son

Rod

P.S. Please destroy this and show it to no one

It is not surprising that Nellie kept Roderick's letter rather than heeding his request to destroy it.

Nellie, who stayed on in Waterville after the burial, worked diligently on her accounts, which she had never had to deal with before. In June, as she struggled to sort through a mass of bills and other financial obligations, she received a blow which rocked her usual composure.

At the Tower Estate offices in Philadelphia, it was discovered that William A. Rossiter, a bookkeeper at the Tower Trust, who had also served as Charlemagne's personal secretary, had stolen over $350,000 from the trust over a period of 16 years. The most affected was Charlemagne, whose income checks from his father's estate were reduced by Rossiter's tampering, with the bookkeeper pocketing the difference.

Rossiter's methods were ingenious. According to a letter written by the trustees, Julius Bailey and Earl Putnam, to Mrs. Seaton Schroeder, Jr., a beneficiary of the Charlemagne Tower Trust, on September 13, 1923:

> Rossiter's method…was to take checks for small amounts, erase the name of the payee (except in the case of his own salary checks), insert his own name, raise the amount of the checks and deposit the raised and altered checks (drawn and signed by the Trustees on the Fidelity Trust Company originally in a proper amount) to his own bank account at the Fidelity Trust Company or some other bank where he, Rossiter, had a deposit account…After the checks were returned by the Fidelity Trust Company to the Trustees, Rossiter would presumably destroy the checks, as the originals cannot be found.

What made Nellie particularly anxious was the fact that Charlemagne had served as a trustee of his father's estate during this period, along with Julius A. Bailey and Earl Putnam, Charlemagne's brother-in-law, who was married to his sister Grace. All of the trustees could be held libel for the missing funds.

Charlemagne's sister Grace, of course, was faced with the same problem because her husband was a trustee. If the two other sisters, Henrietta Wurts, who lived in Rome and Emma Reilly, who spent most of the year in Paris, chose to take legal action against the trustees for negligence it would, at the very least, delay the settlement of Charlemagne's estate. At worst, it would mean a costly lawsuit.

Emma Reilly and Henrietta were very upset about the Rossiter affair, Emma in particular. Nellie felt that she had to do something immediately to dissuade the sisters from taking action against the trustees. She doubted that she could pacify Emma by letter so she booked a passage to Le Havre and stayed at Emma's hotel in Paris where she could see her sister-in-law every day. At the same time she would be able to economize on her own living expenses, as one could live well in postwar France for considerably less than in the United States.

Nellie wrote to Rod from Paris on November 10, 1923. He and Flora had had a baby boy, Whitney, and moved back east. Rod was working on Wall Street; he and Flora were living at the Whitney's estate at Old Westbury, Long Island, awaiting the completion of a house which Flora's parents were building for them on their estate:

> Dearest Roderick,
>
> My life goes on here very comfortably and full of small interests. I went with Aunt Emmie motoring in the Bois recently and again to the Cinema to see *Cyrano de Bergerac*.
>
> I am extremely comfortable here in this hotel but the weather has already grown dark and very rainy and chilly. I may decide to go South to the Riviera for the winter months, but probably not until after Christmas. I will of course keep you informed so you will always know my change of base in advance.
>
> Yesterday morning I had a very interesting interview with Mr. Saul [the attorney for the trustees who went to Paris to talk to Emma Reilly and Nellie about the effect of the Rossiter theft on the Tower Trust and then probably went to Rome to see Henrietta Wurts], who made upon me an excellent impression. He had just seen Aunt Emmie and had, I believe, done much to calm her. She was relieved, on the whole…her excitement is calming down, I am glad to say.
>
> Mr. Saul intends to see you all upon his return home the end of this month and he will tell you things which are scarcely safe to mail, but, the general situation looks favorable for our side, the Trustees. The other heiresses [Emma and Henrietta] will not fight it as they first thought…

Dominie wrote me in a recent letter in answer to my repeated inquiries that you four children had paid for the poor cousins[1] without taking anything from me. I am so grateful to you for this and think it is really touching showing such a tender love for me and father. I have told Dominie to begin the payments from my funds, my share, one quarter of the whole, on Dec. 1st.

I have sent Dominie a check for $2500 to pay my income tax…Except for driblets, I have not much left—it has been eaten up by claims of one kind or another—I must live very carefully, but I insist upon cheerful surroundings and I am spending nothing beyond my actual living…

Your life is certainly ideal now in every way—quite perfect and your bright, happy nature responds so well to it all.

I can imagine how very lovely the babies are—Pam is so unusually attractive and so full of force and vitality.

Give so much love to Flora and with a heart full for yourself.

Devotedly,

Mother

Later—Monday morning—

I cannot make up my mind to close this letter without a word to you on a subject very close to my heart and almost daily thoughts.

Will you not ask Dominie and Barbara to go over some day to see you and Flora in your home with the children?

Remember they have never seen Pam and they look upon the arrival of the first Tower boy as a great event in the family. They need only remain a half hour, if you prefer but I can well imagine the life long satisfaction it will be to them.

They have never written a word, but I know how they must feel and the joy it would be to them especially to see Whitney, for even I am eager for it way over here!

Life is short at best.

It now seemed to Nellie that her plan for keeping Emma and Henrietta from bringing a lawsuit against the trustees of the Tower Estate had worked. With a sense of relief she wrote to Geoffrey on December 7, 1923:

I had a very nice little dinner recently with Aunt Emmie in her private sitting room. We had the nicest visit we have had since my being here, principally because she has ceased talking on the subject of "money loss" and seemed more interested in me and my affairs.

---

1.   Cousins of Malvina Tower, Charlemagne's mother.

I expect to go to Cannes after the New Year. Therefore, address me from now on c/o Morgan & Hayes as formerly. I am undecided what I shall do after that, but I do not expect to return to Paris.

Whether or not I go home in Spring or wait until the Autumn will depend so much upon news from you all and how you feel about my not going to the Homestead for another year.

I do not want to hurry home, open the place for you and then have you prefer living in Quebec for the summer! On the other hand, it will seem a very long time to wait to see you all and sometimes I feel I should rather go in Spring...

I am very contented here and as I have not thought of coming to Europe, perhaps ever again, it seems to me it is best to remain as long as it means anything to me and I shall thus get ahead a little also in my finances.

Thus far it has been a dark and rainy winter. I have many interests and my time passes with very great contentment.

Do not think of me as sad or lonely on Christmas day for I shall not be either. Last year we had such a sweet holiday and all went to church together. So much love to dear Hester—and your very dear self—

Lovingly, Mother

According to an article in the Philadelphia *Bulletin* on April 2, 1924, Rossiter was arrested in Kingston, Jamaica and taken to New York. Presumably the Tower Estate was able to recover some of the stolen money.

Nellie was on a Canadian Pacific cruise, traveling around the world on the *S.S. Empress of Canada*, possibly paid for by her traveling companion, a Mrs. Helwig, when she mailed a letter to Helen on March 20, 1924:

Dearest Hensie,

I am sending you a few lines and a post card so that you can follow me along....

I am sending Bobbie an elephant post card. I am so happy that he likes his "Borneo" book—I often think longingly of him and feel so happy that each day brings me nearer to you all.

Our three days on the Island of Ceylon were most beautiful in the perfect sunshine, brilliant colors of the flowers, very wonderful trees and all the splendor of the tropics. We spent one night in the mountains and it was so lovely after the weeks on the sea.

I am so in love with India and hope to return some day when I can see many of the more interesting things in the interior of this vast country. The natives all seem so happy and are so very picturesque going about in their bright colors with always lots of children.

I have not made any change in my black [Nellie wore black in winter and white in summer because she was in mourning], but I will have to soon for as we arrive at the tropics. The heat will be far greater. Thus far except on the trains, we have never been uncomfortable.

The Aunties [Nellie's sisters, Ada, Floie and Gertrude] write me that you look so well and seem so happy. This rejoices my heart. You, Bobbie and California sunshine seem to be the goal of my long journey. I shall not want to hurry away from you—we are very sure to remain several weeks in Honolulu for it would seem wise and sensible. We might remain several months, so do go away if you still are planning it, irrespective of me—I am bound to be very uncertain especially as I may decide with Mrs. Helwig for what she prefers.

But, on the other hand, I think we are likely to stay in or near San Francisco when once we arrive and not go South for the present.

After another two months on the steamer I shall want to unpack and settle down somewhere for a time—of course that may be in Honolulu.

I am so glad Robby seems so well.

So much love to you all dear—the sightseeing trips are so tiresome but the things we see are so beautiful I have a girlish joy in that part of it which compensates.

Devotedly, Mother

We know little about the next years of Nellie's life. In April of 1925, Flora and Rod were divorced. Flora took the children to France for a year.

Helen and Robby had a baby girl, Gertrude, born on May 11, 1926.

On December 2, 1926, Nellie, in San Francisco, wrote to Geoffrey who had moved to Sugartown, Pennsylvania, near Philadelphia:

Dearest Geoffrey,

Thanks dear for your airmail letter containing such good news about yourself. I am so happy that everything is going so well with you and that you begin to feel really at home in your return to Philadelphia, taking part in the life.

I beg you to be careful and not be precipitate about moving in to the new house too soon. If only I could be there to help you—Is Mr. Parks Terry coming back to buy the bed, etc.? I cannot think of you buying bath towels etc. as well as the hundred other details even for a bachelor, but you seem to have shown so much ability thus far—why should I worry?

Roderick wrote me of the delightful evening he had had with you at dinner and the horse show. He wrote also of the possibility of your spending Christmas together—that would be fine for you both unless he decided to come to California...

Everything continues to go extremely well with me and I feel wonderfully peaceful and contented. My friends are so kind and my independence in every way enables me to do each day just what interests me and I assure you I find plenty to do for others in small ways, but continuously.

My living here in regular expenses is not a high rate but I have still had large bills to pay but I do believe this quarter I can see my way clear to finish up without running behind again. I am so sorry for you in all this work until you can sell some horses. Be sure and let me know how all is going with you financially.

I thank you a thousand times for enclosing those cards left behind in my room. They were important to me in my Theosophical work and as I knew I had left them, I was troubled as to how to get hold of them.

The weather continues to be mild and delightful. I think of you morning, noon and night—so much love,

Devotedly, Mother

On October 20, 1929, Nellie in Waterville wrote to Dominie in Philadelphia:

Dear Dominie,

I am looking over some boxes of "treasures" I found the enclosed record of your Fay School Athletic Winnings—I remember the day so well and of how proud I was of you! You must keep this for it marks achievement and is therefore of real value...

The weather here is so beautiful Geoffrey and I are too sorry to see it end. He will start for Sugartown a week later.

Mrs. Duane's visit passed off charmingly and she too hated to leave with the peace and beauty of it all at this time of year. The Autumn coloring has been so wonderful and with so much sunshine.

I do not expect to go to Philadelphia until a little later and I may remain at Atlantic City for a week or ten days at the Van Dyne when I am alone, or, I may take that time for my stay in New York, returning to Philadelphia in time to be of use to Geoffrey—Barbara's offer was very kind and there may be work for us all to do—[helping Geoffrey get settled in his new house] The furniture is in storage.

Love to Barbara
Fondly Mother

These final letters give a picture of Nellie's life in late widowhood. When she went to California, she visited Helen, Robby, and their children in Santa Barbara and her sisters and old friends in the San Francisco area. She spent summers at the Homestead in Waterville, where Geoffrey would visit for a good part of the summer, and her other children would come for shorter stays. She often invited friends to visit her there. In Philadelphia, Nellie was near Dominie and Barbara and her many Philadelphia friends. Rod was not far away in New York

Nellie celebrated her seventieth birthday on Sept. 2, 1928, at the Homestead in Waterville.

Three years later, in mid-February 1931, she was hospitalized with severe stomach pains. The diagnosis was stomach cancer. She died on April 1, in Philadelphia's Hahnemann Hospital with Dominie and Barbara, Geoffrey, Rod, and Helen at her bedside.

Nellie was cremated, according to directions in her will: "in whatever part of the world I happen to be at the time of my death and I direct that no ashes there from are to be saved." Her memorial service was held in Waterville on April 3; her name, with the dates of her birth and death were inscribed on the back of Charlemagne's monument, facing the marble cross marking Gertrude's grave.

Nellie's obituary in Philadelphia papers read, in part, :

> Mrs. Charlemagne Tower, whose husband was Ambassador of the United States to Germany, Austria-Hungary and Russia, died last night at Hahnemann Hospital, after a long illness...
>
> The Charlemagne Towers were social leaders here and in Europe and lived here many years. Mrs. Tower was a member of the Acorn Club, the Sedgely Club, the Art Alliance, Daughters of the American Revolution, and the National Society of Colonial Dames.
>
> Mrs. Tower was a leader in European diplomatic and social circles while her husband was Ambassador to Austria-Hungary from 1897 to 1899, then to Russia, and finally to Germany from 1902 to 1908. The German Kaiser is reported to have referred to her as "the Von Moltke of society," and "the greatest social leader of my reign." He broke a precedent by dining at the American Embassy at Berlin, sitting at the right of Mrs. Tower...

At her death, Nellie left a small estate that included the $25,000 in liquid assets that Charlemagne had left her, proving that she was as good at economizing in her later years as she had once been at spending.

Under the terms of her will, Geoffrey inherited the Homestead in Waterville. Nellie's daughter, Helen, inherited her jewelry; Roderick received all of his father's medals, awards and honorary degrees, as well as six items from the Homestead or the storage in Philadelphia. Dominie was left only $500, although his wife, Barbara, received a small cash bequest. This suggests that the lawsuit resulting from Dominie's secret marriage to Georgeanna Burdick when he was a student at Yale had been very expensive for Charlemagne, and that it may have been agreed in the family that he would not inherit from his parents. All four children would continue to inherit from their grandfather's, [Charlemagne Tower Senior's], estate.

Nellie had four grandchildren at the time of her death: Helen's children, Abbott (Bobbie) and Gertrude Robertson, and Roderick's children, Pamela and Whitney Tower.

Roderick remarried in October 1932; he and his second wife, Edna Hoyt Lord, had a daughter, Diana, born in 1934.

In 1933, Geoffrey married Annette Tripp Eberle, a divorcée with two children. The following year Annette and Geoffrey had a son, Charlemagne IV, called Peter, and in 1935 a daughter, Helen Scott Tower, (the author of this book).

Among Nellie's favorite possessions was a letterbox, covered with embroidered silk and lined with peach-colored satin. In it were special treasures: several slender books on Theosophy, a prayer book which had belonged to her daughter, Gertrude, and a small beaded purse which Gertrude had been carrying at the time of her fatal car crash. A packet of letters tied with blue ribbon included three letters from Charlemagne and two from her father.

Also in the letterbox was the Japanese fan with the tassels and slender bamboo sticks attached to the handle that Charlemagne had given her in Victoria on their trip home from Alaska. Tucked in a corner of the box was a small diary, bound in red ribbon, in which Nellie had recorded her Alaskan trip, when she met Charlemagne on board the *Olympian*. He became the most important person in her life.

Nellie Smith Tower
1858–1931

Bibliography

Bridges, Hall, *Iron Millionaire, the Life of Charlemagne Tower*, Philadelphia, University of Pennsylvania Press, 1952.

Dennett, Tyler, *Roosevelt and the Russo-Japanese War, A critical study of American policy in Eastern Asia in 1902-5, based primarily upon the private papers of Theodore Roosevelt*, Gloucester, Massachusetts, Peter Smith, 1925. Reprinted 1959 by permission of Doubleday and Company, Inc.

Dolmetsch, Carl, *"Our Famous Guest" Mark Twain in Vienna*, Athens, Georgia, University of Georgia Press, 1992.

Findling, John E., *Dictionary of American Diplomatic History*, Second Edition, New York, Greenwood Press, 1989.

Hagerman, Herbert J., *Letters of a Young Diplomat*, Santa Fe, New Mexico, The Rydal Press, 1937.

Massie, Robert K., *Nicholas and Alexandra*, New York, Atheneum, 1967.

Tower, Charlemagne, *Essays Political and Historical*, Philadelphia, Pennsylvania, J.B. Lippincott Co. 1914.

0-595-34384-8